Chantal Coady

THE CHOCOLATE

COMPANION

A CONNOISSEUR'S GUIDE TO
THE WORLD'S FINEST
CHOCOLATES

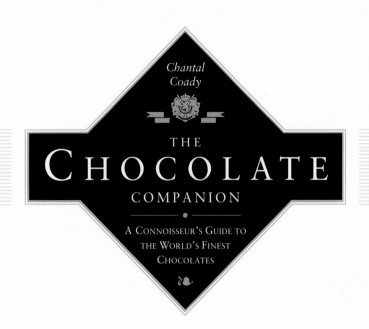

Chantal
Coady

THE

CHOCOLATE

COMPANION

A CONNOISSEUR'S GUIDE TO
THE WORLD'S FINEST
CHOCOLATES

SIMON & SCHUSTER

New York • London • Toronto • Sydney • Tokyo • Singapore

DEDICATION

To James, my husband, and all our kind friends who helped with the chocolate tastings.

SIMON & SCHUSTER
Rockefeller Center 1230 Avenue of the Americas
New York, New York 10020

Creative Director: **RICHARD DEWING**
Designer: **SIMON BALLEY**
Senior Editor: **LAURA SANDELSON**
Editor: **JANE SWARBRICK**
Editorial Assistant: **CLARE HUBBARD**
Photographer: **PAUL FORRESTER**

Designed and produced by Quintet Publishing Limited,
The Old Brewery, 6 Blundell Street, London N7 9BH

Typeset in Great Britain by
Central Southern Typesetters, Eastbourne
Manufactured in Singapore by Bright Arts, Pte Ltd.
Printed in China by Leefung-Asco Printers Ltd.

1 3 5 7 9 10 8 6 4 2

Library of Congress Cataloging-in-Publication Data

Coady, Chantal.
The chocolate companion : a connoisseur's guide to the world's
finest chocolates/Chantal Coady
    p.   cm.
    Includes index.
    ISBN 0-684-80374-7
    1. Chocolate candy.   2. Chocolate–History. .   I Title.
TX791.C63 1995   95-11529
641.8'53–dc20   CIP

Contents

AUTHOR ACKNOWLEDGMENTS

To: Robert Linxe, for his vision and inspiration;
Jessica Rosenberg, whose linguistic skills proved such an asset in researching this book;
Laura Sandelson, my editor, for her patience and encouragement;
Gerard Ronay, who kindly allowed us to photograph him at work;
Kai and Ana-Luisa Rosenberg, for sharing their cocoa hacienda, knowledge and
photographs; and, finally, all the chocolate makers who took so much time
and trouble to send us chocolate samples and information.

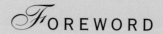

FOREWORD

A large part of my life has been dedicated to chocolate, and I am very flattered that Chantal Coady should have asked me to write the foreword to her book. She is a friend who, I am certain, has produced a book that will encompass every reader's expectations of chocolate—a foodstuff that has become an obsession throughout the world.

Chocolate is a marvelous product, embued with so many virtues: first its energetic value, which can be attributed to the magnesium, potassium, and vitamin A, as well as theobromine, a healthy antidepressant that is uplifting and can be a wonderful way of dispelling gloom.

Then there is the attraction for the gourmet, but this depends on the chocolate being of the very finest quality. Quality is determined by the provenance of the cocoa beans, the manufacture of the couverture, and finally on the creation of fine chocolate bonbons.

To achieve a balance that will satisfy the tastebuds, as much rigorous discipline and vigilance are necessary with chocolate as they are with any field of virtuosity.

I believe that without love or passion nothing great or beautiful can be achieved.

To create a great product is not an easy thing: I have sacrificed much because I refuse to compromise quality: one should never accept mediocrity.

I wish Chantal Coady all the success she deserves for this magnificent book that has involved so much hard work.

With my warmest congratulations and sincere good wishes.

ROBERT LINXE

Paris
March 1995

$\mathscr{T}$HE $\mathscr{S}$TORY OF $\mathscr{C}$HOCOLATE

$\mathscr{F}$ew people biting into a piece of chocolate today would stop to consider that this epicurean delight has Aztec connections and was introduced into 16th-century Europe through carnage, bloodshed, and ruthless exploitation.

In the name of the Spanish Crown in 1519, an adventurous conquistador, Hernando Cortés landed on the coast of Vera Cruz with only a few hundred men, horses, and cannon. On reaching the Aztec capital, Tenochtitlán, they were astounded by the civilization they found there. But only two years later, through Spanish ruthlessness, superior military technology, some heroism, and a lot of luck, the indigenous population was decimated, its wealth plundered, and the centuries-old empire in tatters. Whatever the final cataclysm predicted in Aztec mythology, the Spaniards had meted out a conclusive end to the Aztec Emperor Montezuma's bloodthirsty regime.

Cortés left the smoldering ruins of Tenochtitlán (now Mexico City), with a vast knowledge of the Aztec civilization that he had destroyed, and one aspect that particularly intrigued him was the Aztec's consumption of a strange brew known as xocolatl. Cortés was to introduce his version of the drink to the court of King Charles V. Although Columbus had earlier introduced cocoa beans and the Aztec version of the drink to his patrons, King Ferdinand and Queen Isabella, the bitter, scummy, and peppery drink had been intensely disliked, and the court's attention had been rapidly absorbed by another novelty on the

The Emperor Montezuma.

the dried, roasted, and ground cocoa nibs, and added cornmeal as a basic emulsifier to absorb the greasy cocoa butter.

On ceremonial occasions, large quantities of xocolatl were demanded, often a thousand jugfuls in a single night. Jugs would be mixed from a prepared block of the processed nibs—a crude sort of chocolate tablet. It is clear from Spanish records that Montezuma drank xocolatl as a tonic aphrodisiac. The ladies had to be satisfied by their lord and master alone, for the precious concoction was for men only.

This chocolate was a drink for the elite—it was "liquid gold;" cocoa beans were used as currency and four nibs could buy a rabbit, 10 the company of a lady of the night, and 100 a slave. Given the value of the nibs, it was not surprising that hollowed-out cocoa-bean shells filled with earth were the currency among pre-Columbian fraudsters. Cocoa was grown only on the warm, humid, low-lying Yucatán peninsula to the west by the Mayan people who had been subjects of the Aztecs from about 1200 A.D. Botanists believe that the first cocoa trees grew wild in the shade of the tropical rainforests of the Amazon and Orinoco basins approximately 4,000 years ago, and that they were first cultivated by the Mayans when they migrated to the Yucatán in the 7th century A.D. The Aztecs had imposed a feudal system on their subjugated tribes, and all taxes were paid in cocoa beans.

Santa María's inventory—a Native American. Some twenty years later, Cortés finally caught the imagination of Charles V and his courtiers with the addition of some sugar and vanilla to the drink and stirring tales of Montezuma tossing discarded golden goblets into the lake after imbibing the sacred drink. His success in introducing the partaking of molten chocolate established a new era in the history of chocolate consumption.

The golden goblets of xocolatl that Cortés had tasted at the end of the sumptuous banquets given in his honor by Montezuma were very different from the drinking chocolate we are familiar with today. Xocolatl literally means bitter water, and if you ever have the opportunity to taste a cocoa nib (the inside of the bean), you will understand how appropriate the name is. The Aztecs mixed chilies, cloves, and cinnamon to

Commercial Cultivation

Cortés and his men had gone to Mexico in search of El Dorado (literally, the gilded), and although there were large quantities of gold in the Aztec treasury, they did not find the vast wealth they had dreamed of. Having seen cocoa beans used as a medium of exchange and the esteem in which the Aztecs held the drink as a restorative and aphrodisiac, Cortés put his mind to the possibilities of commercially exploiting this "liquid gold." Cortés established cocoa plantations from Mexico to Trinidad and Haiti. He is reputed to have initiated cultivation on an island off West Africa during one of his return voyages to Spain, and it was from there that cultivation spread to the Gold Coast in 1879. Latin America and West Africa continue to be the principal areas of cocoa cultivation.

When the Spanish first colonized the New World, a huge percentage of the indigenous population fell to the ravages of Western diseases. As a result the Spanish, having already over-exploited the Native Americans as slave labor, were faced with a diminishing population and work force, and the colonists had to explore other means of "recruitment." In time African slaves were to become as important to cocoa cultivation as they were to the burgeoning sugar industry in other areas of the Americas, but during the 17th and 18th centuries, Brazil and Venezuela continued to have the problem of a shortage of labor.

Other important sources of production were Peru and the remainder of the Caribbean basin, but from the beginning the cocoa exported to Spain and Mexico was liable to taxation, for the Spanish Crown was no less calculating than the Aztecs had been.

Mexicans preparing xocolatl, a drink made from cocoa beans.

E u r o p e a n   T a s t e s

An illustration from Diderot's Encyclopaedia, *showing a primitive cocoa press, and the roasting and grinding of cocoa beans.*

For the first hundred years after its discovery by Europeans, cocoa remained more or less the preserve of the Spanish court. It was very expensive and could only have been afforded by those in aristocratic circles, whether in the New World viceroyalties or in Spain itself. This monopoly was gradually broken during the first half of the 17th century. Because of the Spanish Hapsburg connection (the Hapsburg Charles I of Spain had also been Holy Roman Emperor), news of the drink spread to Germany, Austria, and Flanders, and subsequently to France. An Italian, Antonio Carletti, who had traveled to the Spanish American possessions, brought it to Italy in 1606. Reactions were mixed. In countries where it was well established, it was regarded as a wholesome drink, though an early English reference to it by the herbalist John Parkinson labels it "a wash fitter for hogs."

Opinions would soon change, but few people today on tasting the 1640 mixture of cocoa beans, sugar, cinnamon, red pepper, cloves, logwood (a type of fennel), and aniseed would disagree with this early critique. There are even reports of pirates who jettisoned cargoes of cocoa beans into Caribbean waters believing them to be sacks of sheep dung!

In 1660 a Franco-Spanish alliance was ensured when Anne of Austria (Austria being a Spanish possession at this time), married Louis XIII of France, followed by the marriage of María Theresa to Louis XIV, the Sun King. Her maid, brought specially from Spain to prepare chocolate in the Queen's apartments, was nicknamed "la molina" for the "molinillo" stick that had been used since the days of the Aztecs to beat the chocolate into a froth. The taking of chocolate was restricted to the inner sanctum of courtiers, who were invited to partake of a bowl of chocolate during the ritual early morning "levées" (a sort of glorified breakfast in bed). Another major shift in dynastic politics oc-

"The chocolate girl," by the Swiss artist Jean-Etienne Liotard.

curred in 1711 when the Holy Roman Emperor, Charles VI, transferred his court from Madrid to Vienna. The court brought with it the Spanish penchant for chocolate, and Vienna was to become famous for its rich cups of chocolate served with glasses of chilled water and later, of course, for the Hotel Sacher's chocolate cake, the sachertorte.

Chocolate appears to have reached London in about 1650, spreading quite rapidly during the reign of the merry monarch, Charles II, while acquiring a reputation as a nourishing drink. Pepys mentions it in his diary notes for April 24, 1661 as a hangover cure on the morning after the coronation of the king. One of the king's physicians, Henry Stubbe, wrote about the benefits of chocolate. He indicates that even then there were two varieties: ordinary and royal. Royal chocolate contained a high percentage of cocoa and relatively little sugar.

By the 1660s, with the omission of most of the spices, chocolate as drunk by the Spanish and English courts bore some resemblance to our current conception of it, albeit a rather greasy one. In Spain, 1 ounce of chocolate, 2 of sugar, and 8 of water were mixed, heated, and then whipped to a froth. Indeed, the modern version of the Spanish Chocolate *a la piedra* (a stone-ground drinking chocolate in tablet form) contains maize or rice flour, as favored by the Aztecs. In France milk often replaced half of the water, whereas English chocolate houses used either milk or egg.

During the 18th century, Europe saw a rapid increase in chocolate consumption. In England at the beginning of the century, only wealthy

Children enjoying a treat of hot chocolate, late 18th century.

people could afford to drink it, as it was heavily taxed, with stiff fines or prison sentences for anyone trying to evade customs officers. This inevitably led, as it had in Aztec times, to adulteration: starch, cocoa shells, and even brick dust might find their way into the cocoa. It is sad that in some countries, even today, for commercial reasons you can find bars labeled as "chocolate" when they contain as little as 15 percent cocoa solids. There are few other products where this sort of deception is possible, and I hope that in due course consumer awareness will force a reduction of the large amounts of sugar and other non-cocoa products that are used in some "chocolate" manufacture.

Despite high levels of taxation, the charms of chocolate won through. By 1852 duty on colonial cocoa in England had decreased from 2 shillings (24 pennies) to 1 penny per pound, partly as a result of Quaker industrialist claims of cocoa's merits, and partly due to the large volume being imported. In 1850, 1,400 tons of cocoa were brought into Britain, and by the turn of the century this had multiplied almost ninefold. Not only were cocoa and drinking chocolate now much more affordable, but they had become big business. Many of the early cocoa entrepreneurs are now household names: Hershey, Cadbury, Fry, and Rowntree to name but a few. They all owe a debt to Swiss pioneer inventors such as Cailler, Suchard, Peter, Nestlé, Lindt, and Tobler.

Founding fathers of the Swiss chocolate industry:

Francois-Louis Cailler

Daniel Peter

Henri Nestlé

Rudolphe Lindt

The American Market

Big business has always been a feature of the American chocolate industry. First news of chocolate in North America seems to have been in the middle of the 18th century. We know for certain that in 1765 the first factory was set up in Massachusetts by Dr. James Baker and John Hannon. Baker's grandson, Walter, established the Walter Baker Company in 1780, and "Baker's" remains a word for quality chocolate in the U.S. On the West Coast, however, Ghirardelli is the byword. From humble beginnings supplying groceries to the gold rush hordes, Domenico Ghirardelli later specialized in chocolate. By 1885 he was importing the huge amount of 200 tons of cocoa beans annually for his California Chocolate Manufactory. The buildings in Ghirardelli Square remain a famous landmark for tourists, and there is an antique production facility still working there.

However, for the U.S. as a whole, it is the Quaker Milton Hershey's chocolate that is probably best known. In fact, Hershey was not directly involved in chocolate at the outset of his business career, being the caramel king of the East Coast. Influenced perhaps by the chocolate stands at the World's Columbus Exposition of 1892 (an exhibition to celebrate the 400th centenary of Columbus's landing in the New World), he decided that he would make chocolate the snack food of the future. He sold his caramel factory for one million dollars and built a village and chocolate bar factory at Hersheyville, modeled on Cadbury's Bournville in Birmingham, England. Ever the visionary entrepreneur, Hershey introduced a milk chocolate bar with almonds and was the first person to experiment with the use of solid vegetable fats which raised the melting point of a chocolate bar so that it could still be sold in the tropical heat of an American summer or even shipped to the troops as daily rations during World War II. For this reason one might condone the innovation, though it is not an excuse currently available to the industrial chocolate giants of Europe and particularly Britain.

Ghiradelli's bittersweet chocolate and cocoa currently available.

European Inventions

The Americans were relying on the enormous technological advances that had taken place in Europe as the industrial revolution gathered pace. For chocolate the crucial invention was Van Houten's cocoa press, which was granted a patent by Wilhelm I of Holland in 1828. A similar device, illustrated in Diderot's *Encyclopaedia*, predates Van Houten, and shows a machine with a large wooden screw that pressed the cocoa butter out of the chocolate liquor leaving behind cocoa powder, but it was Van Houten who had the commercial sense to patent the invention. Holland and the Low Countries had been involved with cocoa since it had appeared in Europe, and Van Houten's advance, together with the development of the process known as "dutching" (adding potash to lighten the color and make the cocoa dissolve more readily in milk or water) established the

Rudolphe Lindt's conching machine.

Dutch at the forefront of chocolate production. It seems that the English were initially dismayed at the invention, believing that the cocoa butter was an important element in the nutritional profile of cocoa, but they had soon purchased machines from Holland and started marketing the refined powder as the "pure, unadulterated extract" of cocoa.

It was not long before several manufacturers started making eating chocolate. Many people claim to have been the first to have hit upon the idea of recombining the pressed cocoa butter with the cocoa powder to make a solid bar. In retrospect it is strange that Van Houten's invention predated the first bar, because it is perfectly possible to make eating chocolate without first pressing out the cocoa butter. Cocoa had been an ingredient in other sweetmeats long before the advent of Cadbury's French Eating Chocolate in 1842, priced at 2 shillings a bar. Milk chocolate was still a little way off. It was eventually the Swiss who hit upon the idea. Henri Nestlé had been experimenting with a condensed milk to go with his company's breakfast cereal when his partner Daniel Peter tried combining this new form of milk with cocoa, cocoa butter, and sugar. The result, marketed as "Peter's," remained the benchmark milk chocolate in Europe for many years.

Quaker Industrialists

The Cadbury family was one of the four great Quaker families (the Frys, Terrys, and Rowntrees are the others) who became involved with cocoa, primarily because they saw it as a flourishing and healthy alternative to the menace of Dutch gin. These families played a large part in extending the consumption of cocoa and chocolate beyond the rich and aristocratic, making it a food of the people. The drink was promoted as a wholesome "flesh-forming" substance, and certainly with its history as a restorative and tonic, this seems to be a valid enough claim, even if it rings a little odd to our ears today. Another extraordinary element in what these Quaker industrialists were offering was the provision of model working environments and housing for their workers as part of their campaign for more justice and humanity in society. As non-conformists to the established church, the Quakers had been barred from the great universities of the day, and from medicine and law. Industry provided an outlet for their enormous energy, and subsequently their profits were used to air the Quaker views on labor reform on a wider scale. It was ironic that much of this profit was derived from slave-grown cocoa in West Africa, and when this was pointed out by a journalist in 1908, a celebrated libel trial began. The Cadburys won derisive damages of a farthing, but the affair did eventually lead to some improvement in working conditions on the plantations.

An early advertisement for Fry's Pure Cocoa.

The Magic of Chocolate

Throughout the closing years of the 19th century and during the present century, chocolate has grown to be an integral part of the daily culture of all levels of society in the Western world. The very word conjures up warm, comforting images, never more so than in wartime. From the Boer War of the 1890s onward through the two world wars, morale of troops and population was maintained by the chocolate ration. Who has not read Roald Dahl's *Charlie and the Chocolate Factory* without in some way empathizing with the starving Charlie Bucket as he bites into his bar of Fudge Mallow Delight, and finally goes on his voyage of discovery and triumph in the heart of Willy Wonka's magical world of chocolate?

THE MAKING OF CHOCOLATE

The Cocoa Tree

Linnaeus classified the cocoa tree *Theobroma cacao,* which is an indication of the spell that chocolate was able to cast over even a hardened scientist, for the word Theobroma means "food of the gods"—no dry appellation for sure. Perhaps Linnaeus had in mind the role of cocoa in Aztec ritual, its impressive list of mineral ingredients, or even its reputed aphrodisiac qualities. Had he foreseen the modern generation binging on the sugar-laden "chocolate" candy bar, who knows what label he would have given it?

The cocoa tree, a native species of the Amazon rainforests, grows in the tropics, in a belt approximately 20 degrees north and south of the equator. To thrive it needs sunshine and warmth, and young trees must be sheltered from the full heat of the sun and above all from the wind. A great problem of cultivation in the Caribbean is the hurricanes that regularly strike the area, for one day of wind can leave a cocoa plantation fruitless for years. On modern plantations the rows of cocoa trees are often mixed with coconut palms and banana trees that provide shade. This also has the effect of limiting the height of the trees to about 20 feet, making the harvest easier.

In favorable conditions, both fruit and flowers may be carried throughout the year. A small percentage of the tens of thousands of flowers give rise to fruit—the pods that contain the seeds we call cocoa beans. The pods are the shape of a miniature football and may grow up to 12 inches long and 5 inches across, and turn a deep red or yellow color when ripe. For commercial purposes there are two main annual harvests. The first starts toward the end of the rainy season and continues through to the beginning of the dry season, and a smaller second harvest takes place at the start of the following rainy season. The pods have to be cut carefully from the tree with machetes, ensuring that no damage is done to the tree itself because disease can easily be introduced into small cuts in the bark. This is labor-intensive work and generally very poorly rewarded.

(Center) *Ripe cocoa pod.*

F r u i t s   o f   t h e   H a r v e s t

The harvested pods are sliced open revealing rows of fleshy white fruit. The fruit is placed in vats and the high sugar content of the flesh precipitates fermentation. The fleshy pulp surrounding the seeds turns into acetic acid that evaporates, leaving behind the fermented light brown, "green" cocoa beans, which are about the size of a fat almond and look a bit like litchi nuts. This is the process in which characteristic chocolate "notes" are developed, a process similar to that of the fermentation of grapes in wine making.

After this first step in preparing the beans for transportation, the second is drying, which is

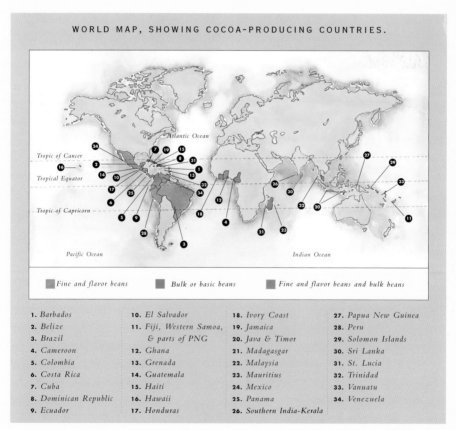

WORLD MAP, SHOWING COCOA-PRODUCING COUNTRIES.

Fine and flavor beans   Bulk or basic beans   Fine and flavor beans and bulk beans

1. Barbados	**10.** El Salvador	**18.** Ivory Coast	**27.** Papua New Guinea
2. Belize	**11.** Fiji, Western Samoa,	**19.** Jamaica	**28.** Peru
3. Brazil	& parts of PNG	**20.** Java & Timor	**29.** Solomon Islands
4. Cameroon	**12.** Ghana	**21.** Madagasgar	**30.** Sri Lanka
5. Colombia	**13.** Grenada	**22.** Malaysia	**31.** St. Lucia
6. Costa Rica	**14.** Guatemala	**23.** Mauritius	**32.** Trinidad
7. Cuba	**15.** Haiti	**24.** Mexico	**33.** Vanuatu
8. Dominican Republic	**16.** Hawaii	**25.** Panama	**34.** Venezuela
9. Ecuador	**17.** Honduras	**26.** Southern India-Kerala	

Extracting ripe cocoa from its pod.

*Cocoa beans fermenting
under banana leaves.*

best done naturally in the open air, sometimes with rolling covers (like those used on tennis courts) to protect from sudden rain. In some areas, especially where there is unpredictable rainfall, the beans will be dried in ovens, but there is always some danger of contamination from wood smoke or the fumes of other fuel, as cocoa beans very easily pick up foreign flavors. Valrhona, the specialist producer in the Rhône Valley in France, will not buy beans that have been oven-dried because their smoky taste can be so pervasive that even a tiny number of smoky beans can ruin a whole batch of chocolate. The dried beans, whose weight will have now

*Fermented and dried cocoa
beans in a sack ready for shipping.*

dropped to a quarter of the harvest weight, are packed into 110-pound sacks ready for shipment.

It is worth remembering that today cocoa, like coffee, is an internationally traded commodity. The vast bulk of the world's production is handled by a few multinational companies, and for this reason only a handful of specialist producers can keep complete control of the quality of the beans they use by sourcing the best beans on the best plantations. The quality and price of their finished products reflect this commercial situation and invariably you will get what you pay for.

The Chocolate Factory

On arriving at the chocolate factory, the beans are carefully checked and sorted. They are sometimes dried again to eliminate the residual 10 percent or so moisture and will then, like coffee, be carefully roasted to develop their flavor. Again, as with coffee, the poorer quality beans will be roasted at higher temperatures to disguise their inadequacies. Each batch of beans that is to be used in a particular blend of chocolate is roasted separately. Even the mass producers of cheap chocolate use a blend of beans, sometimes called a *cuvée*, to create their particular taste, and the process is similar to blending two or more grape varieties to make a wine, or blending malts to make a whiskey. Unlike wine or whiskey, however, it is almost unheard of to use a single bean to make chocolate. Another term that has been borrowed from the wine industry is *cru,* which literally means growth and, as with champagne, refers to a particular, usually good-quality plantation. "Grand Cru," a term first coined by Valrhona, the specialist chocolate

producer in the Rhône Valley in France, is an extension of this idea, meaning a plantation producing the very finest cocoa beans. Certainly Valrhona's Grand Cru chocolates are made with extraordinary care and attention to detail, and their blending panel of twelve chocolate experts meets every day to guarantee the consistency and quality of their products.

After being checked and then roasted, the beans are winnowed to remove their outer skins, leaving behind the nib, or kernel. The making of chocolate or cocoa can now begin in earnest. The nibs are ground by passing them through a series of rollers. At this point the beans will be subjected to one of two separate processes. A large manufacturer of quality chocolate will need extra cocoa butter to add in the final stages of chocolate production and will also be likely to sell cocoa powder for cooking and drinking. Therefore in one process the ground nibs are hydraulically pressed and the cocoa butter melts, leaving behind a cocoa

Cocoa nibs, shelled, roasted, and broken cocoa beans.

Cocoa mass being refined.

powder "cake" which may be further pressed and refined, although most cocoa powder contains some fat.

In the other process the nibs are ground into a fine paste that then goes into a mixer with sugar, extra cocoa butter, real vanilla or artificial ethyl vanillin, soy lecithin as an emulsifier, and milk products if appropriate. The mixer pulverizes and kneads together the individual particles of chocolate that are at this stage, between 50 and 70 microns in size (a micron is one thousandth of a millimeter)—still noticeably gritty on the palate. To make it taste completely smooth and silky, the mixture now has to be conched—a process invented by the Swiss Rudolphe Lindt in 1880. The name is derived from the shape of his prototype, a large shell-shaped vessel, inside which granite rollers further grind the chocolate to a smooth, velvety texture where the particle size is now 18–20 microns, which is indiscernible to the palate. Conching also helps to take away any remaining bitterness by aerating the chocolate. It takes

only 12 hours if commercial considerations are the principal motivating force, although it may take 3 to 4 days if you are a perfectionist. The final step is to temper the chocolate. This involves melting it completely at about 122°F to break down the crystalline structure of the cocoa butter, then cooling it to about 86°F to reintroduce the structure, and finally raising the temperature slightly so that the crystals join up again in perfect chains. The exact temperatures will depend on the type of chocolate, but the effect is to leave the finished chocolate with a well-rounded flavor, and means that it is easy to mold, has a good sheen, and will keep well.

This, then, is the basic traditional process. There are, of course, many variations on it, and many ways of cutting corners and economizing, which will be explained later. Most unusual is an artisan producer, such as Bernachon of Lyon, which does all the drying, roasting, winnowing, and conching on the premises. Quality is never compromised.

Chocolate being conched.

Blocks of pure cocoa butter in storage.

Chocolate Ingredients

Plain chocolate is made up of two key raw materials, cocoa beans and sugar. Partly through the efforts of the producers of fine chocolate, it is in vogue to talk about the cocoa content of a chocolate bar as if it were the only factor influencing the quality of the finished product. It is perfectly possible, however, to produce low-quality chocolate with a high cocoa content; but in my opinion, most chocolate with a cocoa content of higher than 85 percent is extremely unpalatable and the optimum range is between 55 and 75 percent. What is vitally important is the quality of the beans, and perhaps the greatest skill is in deciding on how much sugar to mix with a certain blend of fine beans. Considerations of economy are also likely to affect decision-making, because sugar is five times cheaper than cocoa beans and more than ten times cheaper than cocoa butter.

As with coffee, there are two main varieties of bean. The thin-skinned criollo (the Spanish for "domestic") is the equivalent of the arabica bean, and it is this rarer, less hardy, and lower flavor-yielding bean that represents, at the most, 10 percent of the world's production. It is grown in Venezuela, the Caribbean, the Indian Ocean, and Indonesia. These small trees bear long, medium-sized, deeply-grooved pods that taper to a fine point.

The thicker-skinned forastero ("foreign") is akin to the robusta coffee bean and is widely cultivated in Africa and Brazil. It is similarly robust and lacking in flavor and requires vigorous roasting to disguise its inadequacies. It is this high roasting that gives a burnt taste and aroma to much dark chocolate. The best producers do use some forastero beans in their blends, as they give body and breadth to the chocolate, but it is the criollo that gives acidity, balance, and complexity to the finest chocolate.

It is generally true that when there is less than 50 percent cocoa solids in dark chocolate, it is unlikely to be of the best quality because it will either be too sweet, or fats and other cocoa butter "enhancers" (as they are euphemistically known) will replace a proportion of the cocoa butter content. Why substitute the cocoa butter? Various reasons for substituting the cocoa butter are given by the mass producers, such as improvement in shelf-life or increasing the melting point. One reason is undoubtedly financial, for cocoa butter is valued by the cosmetics industry as a unique fat, melting at just below blood temperature, making it a perfect base for lipstick and other creams. It is this aspect of cocoa butter that gives chocolate its sensual feel in the mouth, and it is something that no other ingredient can adequately replace. If you try a cheap commercial bar, watch out

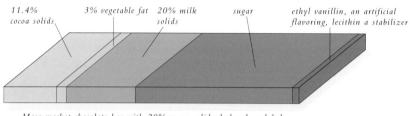

11.4% cocoa solids   3% vegetable fat   20% milk solids   sugar   ethyl vanillin, an artificial flavoring, lecithin a stabilizer

Mass-market chocolate bar with 20% cocoa solids declared on label

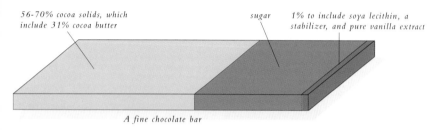

56-70% cocoa solids, which include 31% cocoa butter   sugar   1% to include soya lecithin, a stabilizer, and pure vanilla extract

A fine chocolate bar

Illustration of chocolate bars showing ingredients.

for the cloying, greasy residue on the roof of your mouth—it is probably caused by the palm or nut fats or other cocoa butter substitutes. The cocoa butter's crystalline structure also gives fine chocolate its distinctive snap on breaking, its luster, and its fine sheen.

Dark chocolate with less than 50 percent cocoa solids content is inevitably going to be too sweet. Michel Chaudun, the Parisian chocolatier, points out that sugar is to chocolate what salt is to other foods—a little enhances the flavor, but too much destroys it. One of the problems with sugar is that it has insidiously become part of the food processing industry. Offering little nutritional benefit, sugar is not always used as a sweetener, but rather to improve the overall "mouthfeel" of certain foods.

Another ingredient that has been used in chocolate since Cortés took the drink to the Spanish court is vanilla. It is still used by the best manufacturers, although the majority of producers have been using the artificial flavoring ethyl vanillin, derived from certain species of conifer, since its discovery at the beginning of this century.

The only other ingredient found in almost all eating chocolate today is soy lecithin, which acts as an emulsifier and stabilizer and is added during conching. Its main function is to improve the texture and keeping qualities of the chocolate.

CHOCOLATE STYLES

So far our discussion has concentrated on dark chocolate, because I feel that for the connoisseur it should play a major role in any selection of really fine chocolates. Of course, there is much more to chocolate than bars of milk or dark chocolate, and in this section I will also look at different styles, from the dark chocolate carré to the ultra-sweet cream or fondant. Dark eating chocolate itself comes in an array of styles, mainly characterized by cocoa content, that can vary from the highly astringent and unpalatable 90 to 100 percent cocoa down to unspeakably sugary "sweet" chocolate with a mere 15 percent. As has been stated, however, it is the blend of beans used that is vital. If we make a comparison with coffee, it does not follow that if you put ten spoonfuls in the pot, you will get a better flavor. What you want is more flavor, not necessarily more coffee. For this reason I place Valrhona's Grand Cru chocolates at the top of any list of dark chocolates. Neat marketing ploy that the name may be, it is the standard other chocolate makers aspire to.

Slabs of dark, milk, and white chocolate
couverture from Valrhona, France.

Plain Chocolate

GRAND CRU

This term was coined by the French company Valrhona in 1986 for their Guanaja plain chocolate couverture, which uses only South American beans. They have since developed a Caribbean trinitario chocolate (Pur Caraïbe) and a pure criollo bean chocolate (Manjari). There are also some milk Grand Crus, although I feel that these are better seen as blends of rare cocoa. "Caocaofins" is the French definition of fine beans such as the trinitario and the criollo. The term Grand Cru is still no absolute guarantee of quality, so beware cheap imitations, especially in France. In my experience, price was the only similarity.

BRUT (FDA BITTER)

In the U.S. the FDA describes this as chocolate that does not contain sugar, though it may contain natural or artificial flavoring. Only real fanatics will enjoy this to eat as it is usually intended for cooking. In this category I would place any chocolate with a cocoa solid content in excess of 85 percent, as it is likely to be equally unpalatable.

EXTRA AMER

This is my own category for chocolate with 75 to 85 percent cocoa. This is the upper range for what I would consider palatable.

AMER

Again, this is my own category for anything between 50 and 70 percent. All the Grand Crus fall into this category. Anything much lower than this, and the sweetness will become overbearing.

BITTERSWEET (FDA 35%+)

Unless you are tasting a bittersweet chocolate that has substantially higher than the minimum permitted cocoa content, whatever beans are used will be unlikely to make much impression through the sweetness of this chocolate.

SEMISWEET

This term is used in the U.S., but I haven't come across any FDA classification of it. At midway between bittersweet and sweet, it has approximately the cocoa content of Nestlé Toll House semi-sweet morsels, widely popular in the U.S. for baking chocolate chip cookies.

SWEET (FDA 15% +)

I am always amazed when I hear of bars that are made with such a low percentage of cocoa, which should be the main ingredient. I wonder what else the manufacturers put in. Usually dark chocolate consists of the cocoa solids, with sugar making up the balance of the ingredients. Valrhona's Manjari contains 64.5 percent cocoa and 35 percent sugar.

COUVERTURE

Couverture is the French term for the chocolate used by chocolatiers and pastry chefs as one of their raw materials. The direct translation of couverture is covering, which is ironic, as in the English-speaking world the word is synonymous with the lowest-grade waxy cake and cookie (chocolate-flavored) covering. In reality the cocoa content of cake coating is so low that it bears no comparison with couverture. The French definition of couverture is chocolate containing a minimum of 31 percent cocoa butter, roughly twice the amount found in ordinary eating chocolate. Chocolatiers and pastry chefs choose to use couverture in order to achieve a high gloss when tempering chocolate, for its ready melting qualities and its workability.

In general it is not easy to find "couverture" in grocery stores or supermarkets, as it tends to be used only by professionals. However, if you enjoy cooking with chocolate or want to try making your own, it is essential to find a good source of supply. In my opinion, the finest manufacturer of couverture is the French company Valrhona, but many fine chocolate makers favor Callebaut (Belgium), Cacoa Barry (France), Max Felchlin among others; some even make their own from cocoa beans.

Choosing a couverture is a very personal matter, and the selection available from different manufacturers is almost unlimited. Personally I favor couvertures made with fine or flavor beans (not too highly roasted), natural vanilla, and ones that have been conched for as long as possible in order to remove any residual astringency.

Tasting samples of couverture from Callebaut, Belgium.

Milk Chocolate

Milk chocolate most closely reflects each individual country's chocolate tastes. It has always been a specialty of the Swiss, who invented it, and who still produce some of the finest milk chocolate. Milk chocolate has less of dark chocolate's subtlety, and the blending of the beans does not have to be such a precise procedure.

There are two main types of milk chocolate, depending on what sort of milk product is used. On the continent of Europe, most manufacturers use condensed milk following the original choice of Peter and Nestlé, while most manufacturers in Britain and the U.S. use a milk crumb mixture of milk and sugar that has been allowed to dry out on its own rather than by hot air currents. The distinctive taste of Hershey's milk chocolate, which is known as "barnyard" or "cheesy," occurs due to enzyme activity in the milk crumb while it is drying.

Below is a brief summary of the styles of some of the major producers. In good milk chocolate, we should be looking for cocoa flavor, how well the milk offsets the beans, and whether it melts readily in the mouth without leaving any greasy residues.

Belgian milk chocolate tends to be blander and sweeter than Swiss milk chocolate. A recent tasting of a Côte d'Or milk bar was, to use the American terminology, almost "barnyardy." In France Valrhona have set new standards with their milk chocolate bars and couverture. Fauchon's maître chocolatier, Pierre Hermé, talks about Valrhona's Jivara Lactée as a perfectly honed chocolate that will enable those secret milk chocolate lovers to finally come out of the closet! The archetypal taste in Britain is Cadbury's, which uses the milk-crumb method of production. While not having the cheesy Hershey flavor the best-selling "Dairy Milk" bar has a greasy mouthfeel combined with cloying sweetness. In Switzerland, Lindt, Suchard, Nestlé, and Tobler are world-famous producers, but as a result of multinational politics, Lindt is the only one of these giants that is still solely dedicated to chocolate. With relatively few areas of quality bean production left in the world, I wonder whether these producers are still using the criollo bean in their milk chocolate. Swiss milk chocolate was once famed for its aromatic flavor, but compared to Valrhona's Jivara Lactée, with the exception of Lindt, the Swiss milk chocolate I have tasted recently has not been so interesting. In the U.S. we have already spoken about Hershey as a representative of the American taste. Another American chocolate company is Ghirardelli, better known for its dark chocolate, but its milk is very sweet and a little waxy.

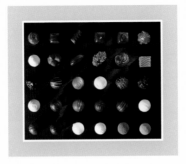

White Chocolate

This is a combination of cocoa butter, sugar, and milk, and it is even harder to tell good from bad. Again watch out for greasiness in the mouth, overbearing sweetness, and a good clean break. Personally I find it difficult to enjoy white chocolate apart from a few rare exceptions, for example when it is used for dipping fruit such as strawberries or cape gooseberries (Physalis). In this context the chocolate balances the acidity of the fruit perfectly.

Organic Chocolate

Pesticides and fertilizers are in general use in cocoa production as in any other type of modern farming, but the main worry for plantation owners are fungi, which proliferate in damp tropical climates. The best protection is the creation of hardy hybrids, but this does not lead to beans with a good flavor. This is why at the moment organic chocolate is made from hardy but inferior-tasting beans. In Britain, Green and Black's produces a line of organic bars.

During a recent trip to Venezuela, I met cocoa hacienda owners and a chocolate producer, El Rey in Caracas, who are considering collaborating in a 100 percent Venezuelan organic chocolate. They certainly have access to the best beans, and it is a matter of time to see if they will be the first to produce a fine cocoa organic chocolate. The El Rey factory is already producing good-quality dark and milk chocolate.

Fillings

We move on now to the different styles you are likely to find in a box of chocolates. This list is not exhaustive because chocolatiers are endlessly inventive. However, most top-quality selections will usually produce a variety including many of these categories.

BOILINGS

These centers include caramels, butterscotch, and fudge and are based on sugar and glucose. Butter and other milk products provide the textural variation while the temperature at which the mixture is boiled accounts for the softness or hardness of the final product. These are very popular in Britain, the U.S., and even Belgium.

CREAMS AND FONDANTS

These are made with sugar, water, and confectionery glucose, and consist of sugar crystals in a sugar syrup that often includes fruit and other flavorings. It is then coated in a tempered chocolate.

CROQUANT

This term literally means crunchy and refers to molten sugar with the addition of crushed almonds or filberts, depending on the country. It is always a shame when peanuts are substituted, a common practice in Britain and the U.S., where the confection is known as nut brittle. The best croquant (Croccante Gentile) I have eaten is made by the Italian company Caffarel in Turin.

GIANDUJA

This is very finely ground almonds, filberts, or walnuts and sugar, mixed with dark or milk chocolate. Often seen in small rounded triangular blocks wrapped in foil.

MARZIPAN

This is molten sugar mixed with finely ground almonds, often flavored with pistachios. It is usually coated in tempered chocolate.

PRALINE

This is very similar to a gianduja except it is usually coated in milk or dark chocolate. This was so popular in Belgium that it became the generic term for a particular type of Belgian chocolate characterized by its sweet whipped creamy center.

NOUGAT

This is also known as Montélimar, named after the French town famous for its manufacture, or torrone in Italy and turrón in Spain. It is a mixture of whipped egg white, boiled sugar or honey, with nuts and candied fruit.

TRUFFLES, PALETS, AND GANACHES

These provide, for me, the ultimate way of expressing the quality of dark chocolate; making the flavors of the chocolate burst out. A ganache is a mixture of chocolate and cream, usually with some butter added. It may be rolled in cocoa powder, powdered sugar, or finely chopped nuts to create a simple truffle, but normally it will be dipped or enrobed in a coating of tempered chocolate. The palet, or *palet d'or*, is like a flat version of this. One way of coating is to dip a circle or square of ganache into tempered chocolate, then flip it onto a marble slab covered with flecks of gold leaf to leave the characteristic two or three lines across the bottom of the chocolate. The particular skill with truffles and palets is in making a light chocolatey ganache whose flavor offsets or combines well with the coating chocolate.

STORING AND SERVING

To keep chocolate in its optimum condition, it is necessary to keep it away from light, moisture, and foreign odors in a room with a maximum relative humidity of 65 percent. The temperature should be 54-64°F. Good dark chocolate should keep at least 1½ years without loss in quality in these conditions and can be eaten long after that. White and milk chocolate will not keep as long, but they are surprisingly robust.

As far as fresh truffles or other chocolates made with cream are concerned, they are eaten ideally within a few hours. In tasting for this book, it became obvious that there is an enormous difference between a ganache which is a day or two old and one that has been kept waiting for two weeks. Truffles which have been made with genuinely fresh cream and little sugar may start to turn moldy after a week, especially if any air pockets have crept in between ganache and coating. The use of a little invert sugar (a product which is chemically close to honey and also helps prevent crystallization) and long-life cream will extend the shelf life to about two weeks.

*There is never any need to keep chocolate in the refrigerator when you have a cool room available. It is however possible to store chocolate in the freezer or fridge, but it must be in an airtight container which has also been wrapped to prevent any moisture from accumulating. **Always** bring chocolates back to room temperature before opening the package.*

THE APPRECIATION OF CHOCOLATE

On first opening a bar or box, check that there is a good chocolatey aroma. It should not have any hint of chemicals, coconut, or overwhelming sweetness and certainly must not smell dusty as this indicates that it is either too old or has been badly stored. I feel that it should also not smell too strongly of nuts, even if there are pralines in the selection. Next we should examine the chocolate. Check the color. It may vary from a deep auburn to the darkest of browns. The finish will depend on whether the chocolates have been molded or enrobed/hand-dipped. In the first case, they will be glossy; otherwise, they have a deep luster. Sometimes acetate film is laid over the dipped chocolate, and when it is peeled off, it leaves a glossy finish.

Gerard Ronay inspects one of his freshly made chocolates.

The nose comes into play.

Place a small piece on your tongue.

Tasting

When it comes to tasting the chocolate, it is best to let a small piece gently melt on your tongue. Unless it is a particularly revolting sample, chocolate tasters do not spit out chocolate because information can be gleaned from the "mouthfeel." Is it greasy or waxy? Is there any grittiness? On the negative side, one should check for any smoky or burnt flavors and that it is not too sweet. Is there a good balance between sweet and bitter? Is the use of vanilla subtle or is it overpoweringly artificial? How acidic or astringent is the chocolate? Finally we should look for a good, long finish as with a fine wine. If tasting several bars, take a sip of water between the different samples, or you can freshen the palate with a piece of apple. Although coffee goes well with chocolate, it dulls the palate in the same way as other strong flavors such as chili or peppermint, so is to be avoided at serious tastings.

Professional tasters often use the same vocabulary as the wine trade. Different "notes" or characteristics are looked for, and compared with fruits, flower blossoms, balsam, even green tea. Certain bean varieties have unusual characteristic flavors, though you will be very fortunate to come across a bar of chocolate with such a flavor.

Snap

If it is a bar of chocolate that you are tasting, break it and listen to check that it snaps cleanly. The crystalline structure of cocoa butter gives the characteristic crisp snap. It should be a good clean break and should not shatter everywhere. If it is a bonbon, you will be able to see if the chocolate has a thick or thin coat or if it has been double- or triple-coated. The current trend in the finest French chocolates is for a fine layer of chocolate to be added to the ganache or praline before it is enrobed. If you hold the chocolate for a few seconds, it should begin to melt unless it contains lots of vegetable fats or your circulation is particularly bad!

Bloom

Bloom is the term for the grayish-white appearance sometimes seen on the surface of chocolate. It resembles the white surface sometimes seen on plums and other soft fruit, though the cause is very different in chocolate. There are two types of bloom which can develop on chocolate. The first is caused by cocoa butter and indicates that the chocolate has become too warm at some point. This makes the cocoa butter crystals rise to the surface, and, on cooling, they re-crystallize. The taste is unaffected, and if necessary or appropriate, the problem can be resolved by re-tempering.

Much more serious is sugar bloom which occurs when moisture comes into contact with the chocolate. This will happen typically in a refrigerator. The sugar crystals are drawn to the surface and dissolve in the water vapor, later recrystallizing. The process destroys the texture of the chocolate, which becomes gray and gritty and although edible will hardly delight the connoisseur.

part two

THE CHOCOLATE DIRECTORY

In compiling this guide, chocolate makers from all over the world were invited to submit samples. The response was really encouraging, and most of the people we asked went to great lengths to co-operate. Sadly, some of the smallest chocolate makers were unable to participate, but we hope to include them next time.

The tasting notes are necessarily subjective, but I hope I have been consistent. As you will quickly discover, I readily admit that I do not like excessively sweet chocolates and find it irritating when a large percentage of an expensive product is made with sugar, one of the cheapest commodities on the market. You might love a particular chocolate selection that is criticized in the directory because favorite chocolates are, after all, very much a matter of personal taste.

The appearance of the chocolates I tasted varied considerably depending on the effectiveness of the packaging that was used. Invariably some boxes had been shaken about, but most had survived remarkably well as testimonies to the individual companies' mail-order departments.

The Directory has been divided into three parts depending on the size of the company: small artisan chocolate makers producing up to 50 tons a year; medium-sized companies producing up to 100 tons a year; and the giants mass-producing more than 100 tons a year.

There were three main categories for deciding on the star ratings of the chocolate tasted:

STAR RATINGS
USED IN THE DIRECTORY

★ *average to good quality, and in many cases, could be improved*

★★ *good to excellent quality*

★★★ *the very best quality available*

the quality of couverture and other raw materials; the condition and freshness of the selection; and the skill of the chocolatier in presentation.

The entries in the Directory can be only a guide, as chocolates may vary from time to time according to the maître chocolatier and the perhaps changing philosophy of the company, so occasional variations, good and bad, are to be expected.

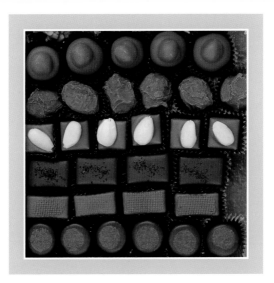

SMALL ARTISANS

$\mathscr{A}$LTMANN $\mathscr{G}$ $\mathscr{K}$ÜHNE

1010 VIENNA, GRABEN 30, AUSTRIA
TEL: (43-1) 533 09 27

$\mathscr{A}$ltmann & Kühne was established more than 80 years ago by Emil Altmann, and since the first shop opened, the burghers of Vienna have beaten a path to their door. At one time there were three shops, though today there remains just one – near St. Stephen's Cathedral in the center of Vienna.

The young maître chocolatier, 32-year-old Leopold Eggenberger, often starts work in the dead of night, making the confections that will later be dipped in chocolate by a team of 15 women. The work is painstaking, as each chocolate is a perfect miniature bonbon that is shaped, then chocolate-dipped entirely by hand and finished with tiny gold and silver balls, perfect whole pistachios and filberts, or with a swirl. The recipes have remained unchanged since the first shop opened, and no preservatives are used. The packaging is designed by the current owner, Petra Heytmanek-Schick, whose parents own one of the great Austrian hotel dynasties. To receive a miniature chest of drawers filled with exquisite doll's house-sized chocolates must be every child's dream come true.

Chocolate-filled miniature treasure chest (above)
and chest of drawers (below).

USEFUL INFORMATION:

STAR RATING: ★★

COUNTRY OF ORIGIN: *Austria*

AVAILABILITY: *From the shop in Vienna and mail order.*

BOX SIZES: *Various gift boxes.*

HOUSE SPECIALTIES: *Miniature chocolates, nougat with rum, fondants, grains de café, and seasonal specialties.*

COUVERTURES USED:
Suchard and Knäbchen

TASTING NOTES:

These exquisitely made, doll's house-sized chocolates, carefully packed in white paper cups with lots of tissue, arrived in perfect condition.

Small cube wrapped in gold foil was filled with a very smooth, sweet, and vanilla-laden gianduja.

Miniature chocolate heart was filled with the same gianduja.

Tiny round chocolate with a silver or gold ball on top was filled with a crunchy hazelnut and coffee croquant.

Pink fruit fondant was very tangy, and much better than I was expecting—perfect for fondant lovers.

Spicy orange gingerbread with white sugar balls stuck on it was very Hansel and Gretel.

Aux Délices de la Tour

1 RUE DES LICES, ANGERS, FRANCE
TEL: (33) 38 98 0029

$\mathcal{F}$ ounded in 1975 in the heart of the historic French town of Angers, this very small artisan business employs five people.

Gilbert Benoit, the 58-year-old maître chocolatier, opened the shop in Angers after running his boulangerie, pâtisserie, and confiserie shop in the Nantes region. Throughout his professional career, while continuing to attend courses at the Ecole LeNôtre in Paris, Benoit's maxim has been to use nothing but fresh, high-quality products, and he is continually trying to find new recipes.

Madame Benoit is relied upon to display her husband's chocolates tastefully in the shop's five windows. Tasteful, too, is the packaging of the chocolates in a small dark brown box with a shiny gold ribbon, simple but elegant.

USEFUL INFORMATION:

STAR RATING: ★★

COUNTRY OF ORIGIN: *France*

AVAILABILITY: *Mail-order catalog*

BOX SIZES: *8 ounces, 12 ounces, 1 pound, 2¼ pounds, 3¼ pounds, special gift boxes also available.*

HOUSE SPECIALTIES: *Le Marbre Amer; Les Coquineries du Roi René; Les truffes Angevines au Cointreau; and Le Plantagenet. Molded clogs and seasonal specialties: St. Nicholas figurines.*

COUVERTURES USED: *Chocolaterie du Pecq.*

TASTING NOTES:

The chocolates have Robert Linxe-style flat tops, and a very thin, crisp fine coating of chocolate.

The rectangular, marbled, full rounded ganache had a good body with a delicate, fresh vanilla flavor and added butter, with a good long finish.

The dark palet with crunchy almond pits inside was the Plantagenet—a ganache with Cointreau—which was very delicate with chopped nuts.

The palet square of crunchy praline had good white chocolate that was not too sweet. The white chocolate with powdered sugar, with its inside layer of marzipan surrounding a ganache, was the least favorite in the box.

Signature ballotin from Gilbert Benoit.

ℬAIXAS

CALAF 9-11, 08021 BARCELONA, SPAIN
TEL: (34-3) 209 13 90   FAX: (34-3) 414 49 84

*W*ithout a doubt, one of Spain's finest producers of "designer" chocolate, Baixas commissioned the artist José-Maria Trias to make a series of boxes based on the architectural, cubist, and surrealist themes that are so influential in Barcelona. Tributes to Salvador Dali and Gaudi abound and form the basis of this series of 15 highly collectable boxes, produced between 1971 and 1991. During the 1972 "Daliana," Salvador Dali himself was presented with a life-size chocolate bust in his own image, and the triangular box of gianduja.

Baixas was founded in 1958 as a pâtisserie by Francisco Baixas and his wife Conxita, and by 1968 had added chocolate making to its repertoire, with the help of chef chocolatier Eugenio Aguilar, who has continued to be "the right hand" in the chocolate production. In 1982 Francisco's son Joan joined the team after training extensively in Europe. Joan worked with Fauchon in Paris and Wittamer

Presentation to Salvador Dali
of the "Daliana" and a chocolate bust of himself.

USEFUL INFORMATION:

STAR RATING: ★ ★ ★
COUNTRY OF ORIGIN: *Spain*
AVAILABILITY: *From selected outlets in Madrid, Valencia, and Zaragoza, as well as some top Barcelona hotels.*
BOX SIZES: *Numerous special gift boxes.*
HOUSE SPECIALTIES: *Fresh buttercream chocolates, Tea Timers chocolate bars with whole almonds on top, almond and filbert chocolates, Neapolitans, giandujas. Seasonal specialties: Christmas turrón and Easter fantasy creations.*
COUVERTURES USED:
Valrhona, Callebaut, Cocoa Cream Caracas, and Guayaquil.

in Brussels, among others, and in 1987 was joined in the family business by his sister Nuria, who took over as traiteur of the newly inaugurated Salon de Thé restaurant in Calaf Street.

Sadly, in the same year Francisco died, but not before seeing his dream of the Salon de Thé realized, and his children continuing the tradition of fine quality and excellent service.

Joan Baixas was made a member of the prestigious International Association of Relais Desserts in 1985, which ranks him among the top 70 pastry chefs in the world. At the Taste of Spain promotion in New York in 1990, his chocolate sculptures of Gaudi's Sagrada Familia in Barcelona and the Giralda in Seville were prominently displayed alongside the famous Madrid landmark, the Puerta de Alcalá.

TASTING NOTES:

The hand-piped Fleur de Lys shape in rich dark chocolate concealed four freshly roasted crunchy golden filberts and was very good.

A chestnut-shaped mold, in rich fruity dark chocolate was filled with a light buttery raspberry ganache, and a maple leaf form was filled with a pale green buttercream center. This, surprisingly, turned out to be fresh mint which was smooth, delicate, light, and refreshing—a most successful combination, and delightfully unsweet.

There was also an excellent dark chocolate and toasted almond cluster; an oval-shaped dark ganache which was very smooth and buttery; a dark log with milk stripes which was a very sweet whipped rum truffle; and a milk square.

$\mathscr{B}$ALDUCCI'S

424 SIXTH AVENUE, NEW YORK, NEW YORK 11011
TEL: (212) 673-2600   MAIL ORDER: 1 (800) BALDUCCI

$\mathscr{B}$alducci's has been one of the great New York food halls ever since it opened in 1948. It was founded by Mom and Pop Balducci, who brought their love of fine fresh food from the province of Bari in Italy. This emporium sells a huge selection of fresh produce, boasts hot and cold delicatessen counters, fresh seafood, caviar, meat, poultry, cheeses, foie gras, and fine coffee, as well as a wide range of chocolates and chocolate cakes.

I sampled the selection made for them specially by Christopher Norman, whose maître chocolatier is New York-based John Downe, who has a background in painting and a love of experimentation. As an artist, he says he blends flavors "just like mixing colors on a palette . . . whatever sounds good usually works." Among the unusual ingredients he uses are raspberry, peach, plum, pumpkin, and passionfruit purée, French lemon and lime extracts, Vermont maple syrup,

USEFUL INFORMATION:

STAR RATING: ★★
COUNTRY OF ORIGIN: *United States*
AVAILABILITY: *From the store in New York. Worldwide mail order.*
BOX SIZES: *4 ounces, 8 ounces, and 1 pound.*
HOUSE SPECIALTIES: *Chocolate Brownies Cake, Chocolate Velvet Mousse Cake, Chocolate Ribbon Cake, Chocolate Mud Cake-in-a-tin, David Glass Mousse Balls.*
COUVERTURES USED:
Schökineg (German)

Balducci's food emporium in Greenwich Village, New York City.

TASTING NOTES:

PILGRIMS PROGRESS: *Like pumpkin pie. It was a fruit, nutmeg and cinnamon white truffle with a buttery texture and tiny speckles of cinnamon, nutmeg, and vanilla.*

LEMON ZEST: *This could be tangier though it had a natural, fresh lemon flavor. The white coating was too sweet and slightly hard, but the fluffy mousse-textured filling was good and a delicate yellow color. Dark chocolate might have produced a more balanced result.*

SUGAR PLUM: *This white truffle covered in dark chocolate powder tasted a little like raisin. The successful plum "mousse" was very fluffy and light with bits of plum visible and the whole chocolate very sweet.*

OOH-LA-LIME: *This half-dark, half-white chocolate, rolled in powdered sugar, had a light green filling of fresh lime.*

MAPLE-WALNUT: *With chunky nut and white chocolate outside and a smooth milk chocolate filling, this was very good! The outside nut texture looked good and was very good to bite into. It was the best and most balanced of all the chocolates.*

fresh mint leaves, eggnog, whiskey and Madagascan vanilla.

The chocolates are very festive, evoking childhood memories and the smell of Christmas. An innovative, interesting collection of chocolates, nearly always successful.

BÉLINE

5 PLACE SAINT-NICOLAS, 72000 LE MANS, FRANCE
TEL: (33) 43 28 00 43 FAX: (33) 43 87 62 85

In 1977 Eugène Béline set up his chocolate production à l'ancienne, using old recipes and methods, adhering strictly to a fine gourmet tradition. Eugène's credentials are second to none; in 1971 he was hired by LeNôtre as their Maître Pâtissier de France, leading a team of France's top 50 pastry chefs who collaborated on inventing new recipes and techniques.

USEFUL INFORMATION:

STAR RATING: ★★

COUNTRY OF ORIGIN: *France*

AVAILABILITY: *The branch in Le Mans and worldwide mail order, for which they have an excellent package.*

BOX SIZES: *9 ounces, 13 ounces, 1 pound, 1¼ pounds, and 2¼ pounds.*

HOUSE SPECIALTIES: *Bugattises: chocolate with praline and caramelized sugar; Les Paves du Vieux Mans: creamy coffee ganache; Les Coeurs de la Reine Berangère: praline and filbert cream; Le Schubert: ganache and almond in Cointreau flavor; Les Mancelles: surfine praline and roasted filbert and cacao; Les Rillettes: the chocolate version of a rich potted meat spread—a special recipe of chocolate with orange and praline flavor.*

COUVERTURES USED:
Callebaut

TASTING NOTES:

DARK CHOCOLATE SQUARES: *The palet with gold leaf was filled with very strong vanilla ganache; another with dark fruity ganache that initially could have been apricot or citrus fruit, but was in fact raspberry, which came through at the end. The square decorated with a plastic leaf was rich and smooth with rum or calvados; and the crunchy nuts and fennel aroma of another made a successful combination.*

ROUND DARK CHOCOLATES: *One filled with a rough almond and orange peel marzipan was very festive; the coffee cream was a good Irish coffee, very creamy and like the drink.*

Other chocolates enjoyed were the flat shiny palet filled with a strong coffee ganache; a rather ordinary dark chocolate crunchy almond praline; and a milk chocolate with a coffee bean on top which, surprisingly, I preferred to the dark chocolates as it was very rich, smooth, and creamy.

The dark chocolate oblong was a fragrant lemon ganache with little bits of lemon peel in it.

Wrapped crunchy chocolate "Bugattises" and rich chocolate spread.

$\mathscr{B}$ERNACHON

42 COURS FRANKLIN ROOSEVELT, 69006 LYON, FRANCE
TEL: (33) 78 24 37 98 FAX: (33) 78 52 67 77

$\mathscr{D}$ eeply rooted in the great culinary traditions of Lyon, the acclaimed center of the gastronomic world, the Bernachon family have come to represent the last great chocolate dynasty. At the age of 14, Maurice ("Papa") Bernachon was sent to be an apprentice pâtissier under the direction of Monsieur Debeauge in Pont de Beauvoisin. At the time, chocolate was a rare commodity, only affordable to the very richest families. The atelier was established in 1955 behind the shop in the Cours Franklin Roosevelt and remains little changed to this day. It would be unthinkable today to set up such an enterprise, with each part of the production from the roasting of the cocoa beans to the dipping of truffles, taking place right in the heart of the most fashionable quarter in Lyon. Until recently, the Bernachons housed their employees in dormitories above the workshops, and even today the company dining rooms feed all 50 artisan chocolatiers.

Behind the glittering series of three shops is a labyrinthine network of rooms; the heady scent of chocolate is almost overwhelming, and there is something tropical about the aroma, a ripeness and volatility. Bernachon et Fils have preserved an almost extinct genre of chocolate making, for at the turn of the century, there were approximately 100 artisan chocolate producers in France; now it seems they can be counted on the fingers of one hand. The most striking thing about the Bernachon enterprise is that although father and son are so fervent about the tradition they preserve, they are also so generous in spirit, they hide nothing, not even their trade secret, from visitors to the atelier, for the provenance of the beans is clearly marked on the sacks of beans. There is an integrity found so rarely in the chocolate business these days. A passion and dedication, a wisdom and clarity of vision has sustained the business. The Bernachons have resisted the temptation to expand because they believe that this would compromise the one thing that is not negotiable—the quality and the control of the quality of their chocolate. They remain convinced that expansion could never succeed for these reasons, everything depends on the unity of the family business, and the abiding presence of real masters.

It is almost unheard of today for a chocolatier to start with a cocoa bean and finish with a chocolate truffle or bon-bon. It is as if a baker were milling his own wheat or a chef butchering his own meat. Almost without exception, master chocolate makers source the chocolate couverture as a raw material and from there proceed to create their own confections. The Bernachons have traveled the world in search of the finest cocoa plantations, the rarest cocoa bean varieties, and most important, the best terroir—that "right" soil to grow that elusive perfectly flavored bean.

In the final assessment, as with wine, the soil is the most important factor, with sunshine and humidity also being crucial. The very best beans

USEFUL INFORMATION:

STAR RATING: ★ ★ ★

COUNTRY OF ORIGIN: *France*

AVAILABILITY: *From the shop in Lyon. Worldwide mail order.*

BOX SIZES: *Numerous*

HOUSE SPECIALTIES: *Truffle Maison, Palet D'or, chocolate cake Président, chocolate bars, seasonal specialties at Easter.*

COUVERTURES USED:
All made on the premises from specially selected fine beans from around the world. Only pure Madagascan vanilla is used. No lecithin is added. The blocks of couverture are aged in a special cool room for three months.

Bernachon's unusually flavored chocolate bars.

come from Latin America, Sri Lanka, and Madagascar. Mainland Africa, although it produces the largest volume of cocoa in the world, is of little interest to such connoisseurs, as the soil is poor, and in general it is planted with inferior varieties of cocoa.

Around 19.7 tons of cocoa beans are used each year in the manufacture of Bernachon's different cuvées, selected from the finest plantations in the world, and shipped via Bordeaux. When they arrive at Bernachon, the beans are roasted gently for about 20 minutes to remove any residual traces of humidity. After this they are tasted, and if necessary roasted a little longer, to bring out the optimum flavor. Beans of this quality need to be treated with great respect; otherwise, over-roasting would result in burned and bitter flavors normally associated with inferior beans. The beans are then nibbed and ground; extra cocoa butter, pure Bourbon vanilla, and sugar are added; and finally the couverture is conched for several days, to refine the texture and to remove any traces of astringency. Milk is added to some of the chocolate before the conching stage; however, the chocolates are predominantly dark.

White chocolate is almost never used except in minute quantities as a decorative finish, and occasionally to make special commissions for babies.

With dark couverture of this caliber, it is hardly surprising that white chocolate is not taken seriously. The cocoa beans themselves have such a force: a tropical fruitiness which positively explodes as the finished chocolate melts on the palate. For this reason, the palets d'or and plain truffles are the most remarkable. Thick Normandy cream is used, together with beurre de Charentes, and these serve as the perfect foil for the rich, aromatic ganache. Filberts come from Piedmont, two different varieties of almonds come from Provence, the pistachios from Sicily, and all the *fruits confit* and peels are made in house, using whenever possible the freshest local produce. The resulting chocolates are breathtaking and well worth a detour from any corner of the world. Failing that, you could always call and have your order air-freighted to you.

Bernachon refuses to expand beyond the heart of Lyon, as they feel that they would inevitably compromise the quality of their product—a refreshing attitude in these times of speculation, takeovers, and mergers. As if to complete the golden circle, Jean Jacques Bernachon has married the daughter of one of Lyon's most celebrated chefs: Paul Bocuse. Who could possibly compete with such a family?

TASTING NOTES:

PRINCESS: *Green pistachio marzipan surrounded a large Grand Marnier-filled center.*

AMANDE-PRINCESS: *Wrapped in green foil, this crunchy croquant of almond brittle with a gooey almond praline on top was enrobed in dark chocolate. It was very very good as it has lots of toffee, but doesn't stick to the teeth.*

PALET D'OR: *Very rich and fruity without the bitterness of the extra amer, this was delicious, as good as the truffle.*

CARAMEL: *Before putting the flat square—half way to being a toffee—in the mouth, the chocolate aroma was very strong, but the buttery caramel dominated in the mouth. It was unctuous and fantastic.*

GUITAR/LANGUE DE CHAT: *This brittle croquant, with lumps of nut, was similar to Gold Cup, but crunchier and more chocolatey.*

PRALINE WITH AN ORANGE FRAGRANCE: *A slightly pitted cross section revealed finely shaved orange peel that had been steeped in syrup. The chocolate was very well balanced and not too sweet.*

OVAL "ROCOCO" MOLDED SHELL: *Filled with a smooth fragrant delicate green paste made from pistachios, this had, perhaps, a little white rum added. It was good and moist.*

MONTÉLIMAR: *A bit bland but very well made, this was not too chewy.*

Exceptionally good were the truffles, pralines, giandujas, and marzipans, and all the nutty ones were fresh and crunchy.

BERNARD DUFOUX

32 ET 40 RUE CENTRALE, 71800 LA CLAYETTE, LYON, FRANCE. TEL: (33) 85 28 08 10   FAX: (33) 85 26 83 56

*S*tarted in 1960, the Bernard Dufoux chocolate shop has grown with the increasing popularity of dark chocolate. Since being voted third-best French chocolatier in 1990 by the Club des Croqueurs, it has been constantly visited by chocolate lovers. Ever obliging maître chocolatier Bernard Dufoux has started to share his professional secrets by doing demonstrations on the first Wednesday or Thursday of each month between 2 and 6 P.M. Tickets may be purchased in advance, and special demonstrations can be organized for interested groups.

Maître chocolatier Bernard Dufoux.

USEFUL INFORMATION:

STAR RATING: ★ ★ ★

COUNTRY OF ORIGIN: *France*

AVAILABILITY: *No branches, but a mail-order catalog is available; also from La Fromagerie, 30 Highbury Park, London N5 2AA, England Tel: (44-171) 359 7440.*

BOX SIZES: *1¼ pounds, 2 pounds, and 2¼ pounds, gift boxes also available*

HOUSE SPECIALTIES: *Dark chocolate palet filled with chocolate mousse; the Chocophile—a mousse with 70 percent cocoa; Truffino—chocolate mousse with rum-soaked raisins; Malakoff—caramelized almonds; Bigorneau—filbert paste with a base of nougatine; Peche—almond marzipan and peaches; Moustache—almond marzipan with pistachio; Antillais—almond paste and raisins; Togolais—raisins and orange; Criollo—coffee; Caramel—made with salted butter.*

Other flavors include: wild blackberry, fresh mint, autumn raspberry, blackcurrant, and "le Green": which is made from fresh green leaves according to the season.

Masterpieces include a trompe l'oeil fois gras; made from chestnuts, and studded with chocolate pieces, laid out on a plate with pistachios, raspberries, and three different sauces: crème Anglaise, a hot chocolate sauce and raspberry coulis.

COUVERTURES USED:
Valrhona with Venezuelan and Caribbean beans.

TASTING NOTES:

The chocolates were excellent, well balanced and full of body, flavor, and aroma, of good texture and with a long finish.

AMANDE AMERE: *Tasting of bitter almond essence, this had a good fruity chocolate.*

CABRION ORANGE: *This orange ganache had good citrus flavor and acidity.*

CRIOLLO: *The coffee cream and ganache were layered.*

PALAIS BOURBON: *This was a very good dark vanilla ganache.*

FRAMBOISE: *This was a raspberry ganache.*

CHOCOPHILE: *This could be a Manjari truffle.*

CHARLEMAGNE

PLACE JACQUES BREL 8, 4040 HERSTAL, BELGIUM
TEL: (32) 41 64 66 44   FAX: (32) 41 64 45 18

ounded in 1987 by Denise Courant-Bellefroid and Jean Francois Staesbolet, Charlemagne was the product of the unlikely liaison of the taste buds of an art and culinary historian and the commercial and management skills of a former endive farmer. They first dreamed up the idea of making chocolate in 1985 following a foreign vacation. Together Denise and Jean Francois have always sought perfection, and have developed the concept of *L'autre chocolat* (the alternative chocolate), which really means using only natural ingredients (with the exception of vanillin) of the highest quality and consistency, taking no short cuts. Each year they travel to exotic places and come back, inspired and full of new ideas and discoveries. The name has been taken from the place where Charlemagne was born in the 8th century, which also happens to be the site of the chocolate production unit today. Charlemagne's royal stamp is imprinted on each chocolate thin.

There is no maître chocolatier as such; however, all the chocolates are created with the help of Denise's fine palate, creativity, and technical expertise.

STAR RATING: ★★

COUNTRY OF ORIGIN: *Belgium*

AVAILABILITY: *From the Pain Quotien group, 20 stores mainly in Brussels. Exclusively from Fortnum & Mason of London under their own label, Hediard in Paris, Embassy in Madrid, and Castellana in Japan. Worldwide mail order.*

BOX SIZES: *24 pieces, 4 x 4 x 1 inch, 7 ounces.*

HOUSE SPECIALTIES: *Boxes of thin flat squares of chocolate imprinted with the Charlemagne logo.*

COUVERTURES USED:

A couverture designed and created in their own laboratory.

TASTING NOTES:

BLACK WRAPPER: *Ginger flavored with a citrus tang, and lots of crunchy sugar.*

DUCK EGG BLUE: *This spiced ginger which was very pungent, had a slightly musty flavor.*

DARK BLUE: *A cinnamon, again with crunchy sugar, had 46 percent cocoa mass.*

WHITE: *An orange flower with no extra sugar, had 60 percent cocoa mass.*

RED: *This was a very fragrant cardamom and delicate coffee with added crunchy sugar.*

GREEN: *Peppermint with no sugar crystals.*

BEIGE: *This spiced Earl Grey tea had no sugar crystals and a 54 percent cocoa mass.*

My overall feeling was that the added sugar crystals did nothing for the flavor or texture of the chocolates, just making them very sweet. Much more successful were the dark chocolate, the tea, and the mint, and the extra-bitter square.

CHOCOLATS LE FRANÇAIS

269 SOUTH MILWAUKEE AVENUE, WHEELING
ILLINOIS 60090
TEL: (708) 541-1317

Le Français Restaurant was founded in 1973 by Jean Banchet, heir to the great culinary tradition of Lyon exemplified by the legendary Fernand Point. Under Banchet's direction, Le Français rapidly climbed the scale of critical opinion, eventually to be rated among the top 10 restaurants in the United States.

In 1989 ownership of Le Français was passed to husband-and-wife team, Roland and Mary Beth Liccioni, already veterans of the Chicago fine dining scene. Roland Liccioni's innovative, meticulous cuisine, although very different from that of Banchet, quickly reassured critics and patrons alike that

23-piece gift box from Chocolat Le Français.

this culinary landmark was in capable hands. Mary Beth Liccioni brought to Le Français her reputation as Chicago's finest pastry chef. She was determined to make Le Français a showcase for the high level of dessert craft that she had learned on her many working vacations in Europe. To this end, a storage room in the back of the restaurant was transformed into a fully equipped chocolate *laboratoire*. There, under the direction of chocolatier Jim Graham, a line of chocolate candies was created to supply the needs of the restaurant as well as a small circle of initiated retail clients.

As word of Chocolats Le Français has been carried across the U.S. by the restaurant's well-traveled clientele and by the press, more and more of its chocolate production is distributed through mail-order sales. All the chocolates are still produced on the restaurant premises.

The maître chocolatier, Jim Graham, is a 37-year-old Texan from Houston who, at the age of 23, traveled to Paris to embark on a career in patisserie. One year later he returned to the

USEFUL INFORMATION:

STAR RATING: ★ ★ ★
COUNTRY OF ORIGIN: *United States*
AVAILABILITY: *Mail order.*
BOX SIZES: *Gift boxes of 11 pieces, 23 pieces, and 46 pieces.*
HOUSE SPECIALTIES: *Chocolate chunk cookie dough and a dense truffle-like cream that can be mixed with hot milk to create a rich, intense cup of hot chocolate.*
COUVERTURES USED:
Mostly Valrhona, though they also mix in other chocolate to balance the flavor.

U.S. to work at the new Houston facility of the French patisserie company LeNôtre. Returning to Paris in 1985, he worked as a pâtissier for the Flo Prestige group. Wishing to specialize in chocolate, he approached Robert Linxe of La Maison de Chocolat in 1986 and joined the team of six chocolatiers working in the original basement kitchen of the shop in the Faubourg St. Honoré, Paris.

During this three and a half years at La Maison de Chocolat, Graham made the acquaintance of Mary Beth Liccioni, then on a "working vacation" from her position as pastry chef at the Carlos restaurant in Chicago. When she and her husband Roland Liccioni acquired Le Français Restaurant in 1989, they invited Jim Graham to assist in the creation of Chocolats Le Français.

Hot chocolate cream, rich and intense.

TASTING NOTES:

These supremely elegant chocolates bear more than a passing resemblance to the greater master, Robert Linxe's creations.

CARAMEL: *A whipped caramel truffle which was melting, smooth, and light.*

PALET D'OR: *This sumptuous chunk of gold leaf on the perfect glossy flat square* palet *had a fruity ganache that snaked along the tongue and melted into the tastebuds with a lingering bouquet and vanilla notes.*

PURE CARAÏBE: *Through the bitter ganache, I felt I could detect a little ginger.*

EARL GREY: *With light flowery, citrus notes, this was very smooth and melting.*

GIANDUJA: *This was an exquisitely light, fluffy cream of gianduja—a roasted filbert and chocolate mixture.*

MOKA: *A light ganache infused with espresso.*

MI-AMERE: *The delicate ganache of milk and dark chocolate was finely balanced.*

NOIX: *A delicate mixture of walnuts and honey.*

ORANGE: *The light fluffy ganache was redolent with freshly squeezed orange juice.*

FRAMBOISE: *The heady fragrance of freshly crushed raspberries, probably the most difficult of all flavors to balance with chocolate, was one of the finest I've ever tasted.*

FEUILLE DE MENTHE: *Fresh tangy spearmint was finely tuned with the chocolate ganache.*

NOUGAT: *Light toasty nuts were suspended in a fluffy nougat.*

CHRISTIAN CONSTANT

26 RUE DU BAC, 75007 PARIS, FRANCE
TEL: (33-1) 47 03 30 00

*H*aving formally trained in the hotel business, Constant was the manager of Maison LeNôtre until 1970. In that year he started his own business on the Rue du Bac, opened a second shop a few years later in the Rue d'Assas, and became famous for his *traiteur* (outside catering) service. He was awarded the Coq d'Or as the best traiteur in France in recognition.

As a chocolatier, Constant's reputation is ever increasing, and over the years he has been involved in research in collaboration with the Institute of Cocoa and Coffee, technical writing on chocolate, writing a book on chocolate for chocolate lovers, and is currently working on *The Great Encyclopedia of Chocolate*. Recently he opened a restaurant at the Palais de Chaillot, opposite the Eiffel Tower.

A great magician, combining diverse and unusual elements from far-flung places, Constant's ganache centers include exotic teas, flower oils, and spices: Yemeni jasmine and green tea, ylang ylang, neroli (orange blossom), vervain, Tahitian vanilla, vetiver from Réunion, Corinthian rose and grape, cinnamon from Sri Lanka, cardamom from Malabar, Chinese ginger, and saffron stamens.

Exquisite gift box filled with exotic-flavored chocolates.

USEFUL INFORMATION:

STAR RATING: ★ ★ ★

COUNTRY OF ORIGIN: *France*

AVAILABILITY: *From 37 Rue d'Assas Paris 75006 Tel: (33-1) 45 48 45 51. Worldwide mail order.*

BOX SIZES: *9 ounces, 1 pound, 1¼ pounds, and 2 pounds; also a wide range of handmade boxes made using fabric and with the collaboration of designer Sonia Rykiel.*

HOUSE SPECIALTIES: *Chocolate orange sticks, ganaches with coffee, plain ganache. A line of special Easter eggs was created on haute couture themes with the collaboration of Yves St. Laurent, Christian Lacroix, Oliver Lapidus, Andre Courèges, Balmain (Oscar de la Renta), Jean Louis Sherer (Mortensen), and Paco Rabanne.*

COUVERTURES USED:

Various, mainly using Central American cocoa beans from Ecuador, Colombia, Venezuela, Trinidad, Tobago, Grenada, Guatemala, Costa Rica, and beans from Madagascar and Sri Lanka. The varieties used are mainly criollo *and* trinitario.

*Box of mixed bonbons
including "two layer" ganaches.*

Christian Constant and friend.

TASTING NOTES:

NOUGATINE: *Made from sesame seeds and covered in a thick layer of bitter, strong, and fruity chocolate.*

PALAIS D'OR: *This was very buttery with a suggestion of rum.*

JASMINE: *The subtle green tea and ylang ylang was very delicate, smooth and buttery.*

VERVAIN: *This almost limy flavor was well balanced and smooth.*

CHINESE GINGER: *This delicious dark fruity ganache had a good, not-too-overwhelming ginger flavor, and even some lumps.*

MANDARIN: *From Sicily, the very strong crystallized mandarin peel was coated in dark chocolate, and I was pleasantly surprised by this confection.*

GANACHE PRALINE: *With pistachio, this had a very fresh, nutty, almost fruity flavor.*

CHRISTIAN SAUNAL

31 AVENUE DES MINIMES, 31200 TOULOUSE, FRANCE
TEL: (33) 61 22 53 42   FAX: (33) 61 13 29 52

The pâtisserie was started in 1954 by Christian Saunal's father, who before this had worked in all the finest establishments the length and breadth of France. Christian Saunal took over the business from his father in 1974. Although it is primarily a pâtisserie, ice cream parlor and, salon de thé, the chocolate side of the business assumes more importance year by year, and Saunal has a repertoire of over 50 types of chocolates and 20 different chocolate cakes.

Born in 1946, the young Saunal spent a chocolate-immersed childhood, as both his parents were in the pâtisserie business. He was apprenticed at his father's side, but also managed to find time to fit in a 3-year degree course in physics and chemistry at the Faculty of Science at Toulouse University. Having completed his studies, he dedicated himself to a career as a maître pâtissier/chocolatier and after a stint in the family business, he went to finish his apprenticeship in

USEFUL INFORMATION:

STAR RATING: ★★
COUNTRY OF ORIGIN: *France*
AVAILABILITY: *From branches: 147 Grande Rue Saint Michel-31400, Toulouse Tel: (33) 61 52 77 12; and Marché Victor Hugo, Toulouse Tel: (33) 61 13 63 20.*
BOX SIZES: *8½ ounces, 12 ounces, 1 pound, 1½ pounds, and 2¼ pounds.*
HOUSE SPECIALTIES: *Their 50 types of chocolate and 20 different chocolate cakes set them apart. Seasonal specialties are marrons glacé.*
COUVERTURES USED:
Valrhona, Cacao Barry

TASTING NOTES:

The Earl Grey Tea ganache was a good example of Saunal's "two-level" ganaches, and was made from Manjari, Valrhona's fruitiest couverture. Similarly the dark round truffle was very smooth with delicate aniseed notes and a very long finish.

Of two palet, the guanaja was a very smooth, buttery dark ganache with vanilla, and Armagnac, a ganache made from Valrhona Caraïbe and Armagnac.

the best-known houses in the region.

When he returned to the family business in 1974, his enthusiasm for chocolate had become a real passion. Since then he has dedicated himself to creating a range of subtle, delicate ganaches that work on two levels: the first notes are floral or aromatic; and the other elements come through more slowly with a really long finish, as one would expect with a fine wine.

$\mathscr{D}$E $\mathscr{B}$ONDT

VIA TURATI 22 (CORTE SAN DOMENICO) 56125 PISA,
ITALY   TEL/FAX: (39) 50 501896

Opened in December 1993 by Dutch pastry chef Paul de Bondt and Cecilia Iacobelli who trained at the Academia de Belle Arti in Carrara, Italy, de Bondt is a newcomer to the world of fine chocolate.

De Bondt trained as both chef pâtissier and chef de cuisine, working extensively in 4- and 5-star hotels in the Tuscany region. His and Cecilia Iacobelli's philosophy is to produce the highest-quality chocolates, using only the finest ingredients, the best couvertures and ganache as a base for the fillings. Specially chosen ingredients include lemons from Monterosso (Liguria), walnuts from Salerno, Sicilian almonds, and crystallized orange and lemon peel from organically grown fruit.

The style of the shop and the exquisite packaging, which suits the original and superbly made chocolates, are contemporary as opposed to romantic. Simplicity is the key word here, reflecting

Tuscan cuisine: fresh, unpretentious, and most certainly one of the world's finest.

I will be following de Bondt's progress with particular interest, as the selection I tasted were quite exceptional. I would go so far as to say that these were some of the most memorable chocolates tasted.

USEFUL INFORMATION:

STAR RATING: ★ ★ ★
COUNTRY OF ORIGIN: *Italy*
AVAILABILITY: *From the shop in Pisa.*
BOX SIZES: *4 ounces, 4½ ounces, 8 ounces, and 12 ounces.*
COUVERTURES USED:
Top secret

TASTING NOTES:

Most were very finely balanced and delicate with excellent dark chocolate and of a soft consistency. They were beautifully made and finished, and their presentation was superb.

HALF-DIPPED CRYSTALLIZED MELON: *This was delicate, beautiful, not too sweet.*

ORANGE GANACHE: *Diamond-shaped with dark cocoa powder, the orange ganache was fragrant with a perfectly balanced taste.*

LEMON GANACHE: *Diamond-shaped with dark cocoa powder, and made with fresh Liguria lemon, this had a fragrant and very natural, good flavor, reminiscent of fresh ginger.*

TEA GANACHE: *A slightly lighter chocolate than others, it had Earl Grey and perhaps a faint hint of jasmine. Delicious!*

GIANDUJA: *The delicious and very distinctive nut taste was very fresh and slightly grainy.*

CHESTNUT HONEY GANACHE: *This had a bubblegum taste and a good texture.*

HAND-ROLLED TRUFFLE: *Dusted with cocoa but quite pale, the truffle had caramel filling. It was smooth and delicate and very good.*

WALNUT GIANDUJA: *With an interesting, slightly sandy texture, this gianduja had a very soft and strong walnut taste—one of the best.*

Other highlights in the selection were the classic white truffle with a slightly heavier, denser texture than the others; a mendiant of pine nuts, almonds, raisins, and filberts made of dark chocolate; and the rum and raisin ganache with its pleasant soft texture and combination of tastes.

$\mathscr{D}$E $\mathscr{L}$ÉAUCOUR

45/47 CHAUSSEE D'ESTAIMPUIS, 7712 HERSEAUX-GARE, BELGIUM   TEL/FAX: (32) 56 843472

The chocolate maker at Chocolats de Léaucour is Jean-Louis Marlier, an illustrator by profession who, 8 years ago, in desperation at being unable to find "real" chocolate in Belgium, started making his own chocolates in his spare time. Knowing nothing, Marlier had to learn or invent everything and, over the course of 2 years, gradually resolved the large number of technical problems that had arisen. He slowly discovered what was required to create optimum-quality chocolates, and the reasons why the quality of industrially produced chocolates leaves so much to be desired. Unusually for Belgian chocolate, no extra sugar is added to the fillings, which has the dual advantage of improving the taste of the chocolate and the health of the consumer. "There is no greater pleasure for a chocolatier than to have a clientele of sportsmen, heart specialists, and dieticians," and he reveals that many clients have said that his Léaucour chocolates suit them perfectly, giving absolutely no headaches or digestive problems whatsoever.

The recipes are, of course, top secret, but becoming simpler and purer all the time. While the nutty pralines are enrobed in a dark couverture containing 55 to 60 percent cocoa mass, to achieve a delicacy and balance, his orange is robust enough to take a really dark chocolate with 75 to 85 percent cocoa mass, and the results speak for themselves.

Small, dark chocolate disks containing 85% cocoa mass.

USEFUL INFORMATION:

STAR RATING: ★ ★

COUNTRY OF ORIGIN: *Belgium*

AVAILABILITY: *From the shop in Belgium.*

BOX SIZES: *8 ounces, 1 pound, 1½ pounds, and 2 pounds. There are about 60 chocolates to the pound: they are about half the size of most Belgian chocolates.*

HOUSE SPECIALTIES: *None as such, but little or no butter is used in pralines, and they are generally flavored with fruit or nuts.*

COUVERTURES USED: *Top secret*

TASTING NOTES:

All these chocolates are enrobed rather than molded. This is unusual, if not unique in Belgium, and is partly done to get away from the industrial mass-produced approach represented by mechanization and economies of scale. The other reason is to obtain an appearance which is both convivial and original. As Marlier explains, this has the disadvantage of being time-consuming and may leave a less-than-perfect finish, but "my customers don't mind because they know they are getting a handmade product."

Garnishes on top of the palet *indicate the center of each chocolate. A further feature is that the chocolates are themselves very small—about 60 pieces per pound, instead of a more predictable 30. Indeed no economies of scale here!*

DELEANS

20 RUE CÉRÈS, REIMS, 51100, FRANCE
TEL: (33) 26 47 56 35

ounded in 1810 by Monsieur Deleans, the business was bought by the current owner and maître chocolatier's grandfather in 1910.

Monsieur J. Gaudon, the maître chocolatier, inherited his passion for chocolate over three generations and has been making chocolates since his early childhood, when he learned the tricks of the trade at his father's knee. After studying chocolate making and finally gaining his Brevet de Maîtrise, he subsequently became a maître artisan chocolatier. He is a charming example of the old-world artisan chocolatier.

USEFUL INFORMATION:

STAR RATING: ★ ★ ★

COUNTRY OF ORIGIN: *France*

AVAILABILITY: *From the branch in Reims.*

BOX SIZES: *8 ounces, 12 ounces, 1 pound, 1½ pounds, and 2¼ pounds.*

HOUSE SPECIALTIES: *Nelusco cherries; Palet Café; almond praline; filbert praline; pâté d'amande.*

COUVERTURES USED:
Gaudon makes his own blend using Valrhona and Callebaut and adding extra cocoa butter and cocoa powder.

FOUQUET

36 RUE LAFFITTE, 75009 PARIS, FRANCE
TEL: (33-1) 47 70 85 00

22 RUE FRANÇOIS-1ER, 75008 PARIS, FRANCE
TEL: (33-1) 47 23 30 36

Since it was founded in 1852, Fouquet has sold a wide range of groceries including chocolates and other confections that are still made on the premises. The store's location in the bohemian 9th arrondissement of Paris attracted local artists such as Gertrude Stein. In 1926 a second store opened in the fashionable 8th arrondissement on the corner of the Champs-Elysées and Rue Francois 1er.

Rigorously keeping to traditional production methods and making no compromises by using cheap ingredients, Fouquet uses only the finest quality of raw materials. Currently under the direction of the fourth generation of the family, Mlle. Chambeau-Fouquet and her nephew, Christophe, Fouquet imports cocoa beans direct from Venezuela and pure vanilla from Réunion. Using only the freshest ingredients and working on a truly artisan scale, small batches of chocolates are prepared

Lavish packaging in true Parisian style.

daily. Handmade boxes are packed with two layers of chocolates, and old-fashioned waxed paper and satin ribbon add the final touches to the packaging.

USEFUL INFORMATION:

STAR RATING: ★ ★

COUNTRY OF ORIGIN: *France*

AVAILABILITY: *From two stores in Paris.*

BOX SIZES: *Rectangular boxes: 12 ounces, 1 pound, 1¼ pounds, 1¼ pounds, 2 pounds; round boxes: 1¼ pounds, 2¼ pounds, 3 pounds, and 7¼ pounds.*

HOUSE SPECIALTIES: *Very hard caramels. Seasonal specialties are chocolate hearts filled with pralines; molded Easter eggs; fish; bells; and an assortment of chocolates rooted in 19th-century tradition of sugar-fondant ducks, rabbits, fish, seashells, and flowers.*

COUVERTURES USED: *Top secret*

TASTING NOTES:

This selection of chocolates reminded me of a fine classic English selection from the Empire days, and especially by the double enrobing of the chocolates, which is much maligned by the new-wave French chocolatiers, but still boasted of by some English chocolatiers.

The double enrobed orangette was not sticky, almost dry, but quite tangy and not too sweet; and a heart-shaped chocolate, again double enrobed, with toasted almond chunks inside was a simple unpretentious chocolate.

The Croustillant with its thin dark chocolate couverture had a crispy, croquant, cookie-style center, which was buttery, crunchy, and very good.

Caramel Café—a soft coffee caramel in dark chocolate was a bit chewy, but very good; Caramel au Chocolat was a dark gooey chocolate caramel, which seems to be the house specialty; and Praline Domino was good if a little sweet.

A very sticky marzipan seemed to be doused with liqueur. Others in the selection were the Chocolate Ginger and the Palet Café.

$\mathscr{F}$RANCISCO
$\mathscr{T}$ORREBLANCA

103 AVENIDA JOSÉ MARTINEZ GONZALEZ, 03600 ELDA
(ALICANTE), SPAIN
TEL/FAX: (34·96) 538 82 24

$\mathscr{F}$rancisco Torreblanca is one of only four chef pâtissiers in Spain to be awarded membership of the *Relais Desserts*. He won their prize for the best Spanish pâtissier in 1988 and the best artisan pâtissier in the European Community in 1990. Torreblanca makes pastries, chocolates, and jams using fine-quality ingredients, free of colorings and preservatives. His chocolates have a shelf life of about 6–8 weeks.

USEFUL INFORMATION:

STAR RATING: ★ ★ ★

COUNTRY OF ORIGIN: *Spain*

AVAILABILITY: *From the shop in Alicante and others throughout Spain.*

BOX SIZES: *Numerous*

HOUSE SPECIALTIES: *Very fine chocolates made with saffron; cinnamon; pear and ginger; coffee; tea; filberts; pistachio; and cinnamon combined with fine rare chocolate couvertures.*

COUVERTURES USED: *Valrhona*

Chef pâtissier Francisco Torreblanca.

TASTING NOTES:

The chocolates I tasted were outstanding, though packed in a bizarre way for fine chocolates—on a cardboard base, wrapped in gift paper.

A FLAT SQUARE DARK CHOCOLATE PALET: *Threads of orange and lemon rind were incorporated in a smooth silky ganache.*

SQUARE DARK CHOCOLATE *PALET* WITH FORK MARKS: *The aroma of reglisse, or licorice, was subtle and finely balanced with the rich ganache and the beautifully fine, crisp chocolate on the outside.*

A SANDWICH TOPPED WITH MILK CHOCOLATE: *A salty turrón made from pistachio with a sweet milk gianduja, provided an unexpected combination of sweet and salt—reminiscent of porridge in a way, due to the texture of the nuts and the saltiness.*

AN OVAL MILK CHOCOLATE: *This butterscotch, caramel, and fragrant Ceylon tea combination was very fine and unusual.*

PALET ARGENT: *This milk chocolate palet, with a silver leaf on top, had inside it a very fine and delicately perfumed almond and milk chocolate ganache.*

A COCOA-DUSTED WHISKEY TRUFFLE: *Wonderful bitter chocolate, combined well with a rich dark whiskey truffle.*

POWDERED SUGAR-DUSTED TRUFFLE: *With praline and possibly orange, this was fine but a little sweet.*

AN ALMOND CLUSTER: *Little slithers of toasted almond in dark chocolate were fine.*

$\mathcal{G}$ERARD $\mathcal{R}$ONAY

3 WARPLE WAY, LONDON W3 ORF, UK
TEL: (44-181) 743 0818

$\mathcal{P}$robably Britain's most feted chocolatier, Gerard Ronay set up his chocolate-making business in 1989. After working as a psychiatric nurse, Ronay trained to be a maître chocolatier with a star-studded array of masters, including Robert Linxe, Jean-Paul Hévin, Christian Constant, L'Ecole LeNôtre, and Bernachon in France, Wittamer in Belgium, and Charbonnel et Walker in England.

Ronay is best known for his eclectic palate, and unusual combinations of English produce blended with chocolate ganaches made in the classic French tradition. He is highly secretive about his exact recipes, although he has let it slip that in his high-security mixing room there can be found exotic and unconventional ingredients such as garlic and balsamic vinegar, so tasting his creations is a real challenge to the skills of the tastebuds and olfactory senses.

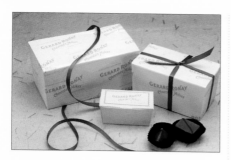

Distinctive packaging from Gerard Ronay.

At Easter the most exquisitely beautiful eggs, hand painted with different colored couvertures, are made, and it would not surprise me to find that many of these works of art remain uneaten. Ronay was awarded the Diplome du Club des Croqueurs du Chocolat in Paris for his Geranium chocolate, a great honor indeed!

USEFUL INFORMATION:

STAR RATING: ★ ★ ★
COUNTRY OF ORIGIN: *Britain*
AVAILABILITY: *From Harrods; Rococo; and Theobroma Chocolates, Camden, London.*
BOX SIZES: *3 to 4 chocolates, 8 ounces, 1 pound, and 2 pounds.*
HOUSE SPECIALTIES: *Easter eggs, hearts, boxes, flowers, and other commissions made to order.*
COUVERTURES USED: *Valrhona, Cacao Barry, and Grossistes de France.*

TASTING NOTES:

These ganaches are loaded with rich fresh flavor sensations. Occasionally the amount of liquid used results in ganache with a grainy texture, but they are usually exceptionally smooth, well balanced, and melting on the palate. My favorite is the tangy gooseberry, with the rhubarb a close second; the dill and rose combine to make a subtle and exotic combination.

For the Garden Mint chocolate, fresh mint leaves are infused in cream and blended with chocolate reminiscent of new potatoes cooked with fresh mint. Certainly it is a far cry from the classic English chocolate and mint fondant combination.

The Tomato is the most surprising. Tasted blind this is probably the most difficult of all to identify, but the fruity slightly acidic notes of the tomato are perfectly balanced by the dark chocolate.

The Tea ganache is another taste challange: some swear it is Lapsang Souchong, others Jasmine, others think it could be Earl Grey. Who knows, except Gerard, and he certainly isn't going to tell us. It is probably a combination of at least five different teas.

Smoked Lemon—a most unusual mixture of woodsmoke and citrus peel has a very good texture; and the Geranium chocolate is the most fragrant of all, again well balanced with the chocolate ganache.

Other chocolates are: After-dinner Bitter, Calvados, Caramel and Raisin, Chestnut, Coffee, Coffee and Cardamom, Date, Orange, Praline, Raspberry, Red Wine Truffle, and Maple and Walnut.

JEAN-PAUL HÉVIN

3 RUE VAVIN, 75006 PARIS, FRANCE
TEL: (33-1) 43 54 09 85

*I*n 1990 Jean-Paul Hévin started the company using his name. Voted second best chocolatier in France after Robert Linxe in the 1994 Guide Juillard des Croqueurs de Chocolat, Jean-Paul Hévin represents the new generation of French chocolatiers. Although he is still in his early thirties, his rigorous training stretches back over ten years, and he has been winning prizes from the very beginning. In 1988 he won first prize for chocolate making and the title Meilleur Ouvrier de France in 1986. He has worked under the tutelege of two former winners of this trophy. Joel Rebouchon and Michel Foussart. Hévin also worked with Peltier and even opened and ran the Tokyo shop for a year. With this illustrious background, Jean-Paul bought his first shop, a Russian tea-house, Le Petit Boule, in 1988, and created a line of serious dark chocolate delicacies.

USEFUL INFORMATION:

STAR RATING: ★ ★ ★

COUNTRY OF ORIGIN: *France*

AVAILABILITY: *From the two shops in Paris, mail-order, also on French Minitel ("3615 Paissio").*

BOX SIZES: *Numerous*

HOUSE SPECIALTIES: *Seasonal specialty: flat Easter eggs.*

COUVERTURES USED: *Valrhona*

TASTING NOTES:

Deliciously fragrant dark chocolates were arranged jewel-like in their caramel-colored box. All were incredibly delicate, and the heady aroma of chocolate made way in due course for fine and subtle fragrances.

MAUBOURG: *This deliciously light praline had tiny pieces of caramelized nougatine.*

ESMERALDA: *The glossy fragrant raspberry ganache finely balances the fruit, which emerges slowly on the tongue.*

GANACHE AU THÉ FUMÉ: *Decorated with cocoa spots, the ganache was so light that the smoked tea almost floats away before you capture its fragrance.*

ZENZERO: *A fruity ginger ganache that had a note of deep black licorice which emerged at the end.*

KEOPS: *This piped succulent pistachio marzipan was covered in the finest layer of intense dark chocolate.*

LE PETIT BOULE: *The delicate chocolatey caramel melted through the ganache, without either element overpowering the other.*

CAPARUNA: *This floral, heather-scented deep chocolate ganache, evoked warm summer days.*

LE 1502: *A dark cream and buttery ganache, which was bitter and slightly astringent.*

JOËL DURAND

5 QUAI CHATEAUBRIAND, 3500 RENNES, FRANCE
TEL: (33) 99 78 10 00

The small shop and salon de thé opened in 1987 can be found nestling in a beautiful baroque façade in the historic town of Rennes. From the start, Joël Durand showed his flair and originality in creating special cakes and handmade chocolates. He found pâtisserie the perfect medium for expressing his ideas, but when he started working with chocolate, his mind went into overdrive, dreaming up all sorts of unlikely flavor combinations, and then putting them into practice. Using a ganache as a canvas, Durand experimented with such diverse flavors as lavender, thyme, black pepper, and cloves to create beautifully rounded and delicate epicurean bouchées.

At the age of 28, Joël Durand is the youngest chocolatier to be voted among the top 10 chocolatiers in France by the Club des Croqueurs de Chocolat. Traditionally every chocolatier has

USEFUL INFORMATION:

STAR RATING: ★ ★ ★
COUNTRY OF ORIGIN: *France*
AVAILABILITY: *From the shop in Rennes.*
BOX SIZES: *8 ounces and 12 ounces.*
HOUSE SPECIALTIES: *Numbered ganaches
with Earl Grey, cinnamon, jasmine tea,
Lapsang Souchong, fresh mint leaves, lavender,
nutmeg, liquorice, cardamom, thyme, cloves,
and Chinese pepper.*
COUVERTURES USED:
*Cacao Barry, and he is starting to experiment
with making his own couverture using beans
from Guyana and the Cameroons.*

TASTING NOTES:

NO. 2: *A milky ganache with a slightly dry
texture and lots of orange zest.*

NO. 5: *Earl Grey from "Maison Damann" is a
classic, made with very smooth milky ganache
which was well balanced and extremely fragrant.*

NO. 6: *Thé Noël was a cinnamon tea from
Marriage Frères (Paris Tea Merchant), blended
with a smooth and subtle ganache, with a lingering
bouquet of cinnamon.*

NO. 7: *Jasmine was fragrant and instantly
evocative of China, fine and well balanced.*

NO. 9: *Menthe Fraiche was fresh spearmint
leaves infused in a white chocolate ganache,
delicate, well balanced, and very smooth.*

NO. 10: *Lavender which was a surprisingly good
combination of flavors; the lavender takes on a
herby flavor, a little like rosemary.*

NO. 11: *Nutmeg, cinnamon, lemon zest, and
Réunion vanilla—very festive and Christmasy.*

NO. 12: *The star of the show—a perfect
marriage of white chocolate and licorice. The gentle
vanilla notes first come through followed by melting
bittersweet licorice notes. Most original.*

NO. 14: *A caramel ganache with strong flavor of
burned sugar; the addition of salty butter adds an
interesting twist.*

NO. 16: *A ganache made with sundried
Réunion vanilla.*

NO. 24: *A black pepper ganache which was
another unusual but extremely successful
combination; subtly pungent and the chocolate
balanced perfectly with the spice.*

his own "signature," perhaps a particular shape,
or set of molds. For Joël Durand it is a number-
ing system—each of his 26 chocolates is identi-
fied by its own number placed on top of the
chocolate palet by means of a cocoa butter
transfer. A menu is supplied with each box for
decoding purposes. It may be a bit of a gamble
when it comes to the 6 and the 9—they looked
the same to me!

JUNCAL

CALLE RECOLETOS NO 15, MADRID 28001, SPAIN
TEL: (34-1) 435 13 55

*O*ver 100 years ago, Doctor Zaragueta, the current owner's great-grandfather started a family tradition: he made chocolates as a hobby and distributed them among his friends and family. The first real shop was opened in 1950 in Irún, adopting the name of their patron saint, the Virgin of Juncal. Then in 1953 the business moved to Madrid, where it quickly established itself as one of the city's leading confectioners. Today Jesús-Maria Zaragueta Elgorriaga continues the tradition, personally overseeing the chocolate production as well as the management, marketing, and packaging for their three shops in Spain; two in Madrid, the third in Bilbao. It is very much a family business and Elgorriaga's daughters (the fifth generation), Marta, Susana, and Juncal, are all dedicated "to sweetening people's lives."

Manuel Humbrados Llana has been the maître chocolatier for over 30 years, and his skills were inherited from a direct line of artisan workers who had trained under Dr. José Gil's and Dr. Zaragueta's direction.

Juncal's signature gift box presentation.

USEFUL INFORMATION:

STAR RATING: ★

COUNTRY OF ORIGIN: *Spain*

AVAILABILITY: *From the shop in Madrid and Juncal-Calle Maiquez No. 3, Madrid and Juncal-Calle Doctor Achucaro No. 4, Bilbao.*

BOX SIZES: *Numerous. Many "fantasy" gift boxes.*

HOUSE SPECIALTIES: *Over 80 types of chocolates including: frosted egg yolks, chocolate dipped toffees, and Vienna liqueur soaked apricots, 25 sizes of Easter eggs, chickens, chicks, rabbits, hares, and bells and Valentine's hearts.*

COUVERTURES USED:
Their own dark, milk, and white couvertures.

TASTING NOTES:

The selection included a liqueur chocolate in white and dark butter ganache with a dark chocolate shell; and a round white chocolate with a black spot on top which was filled with a very sweet and rather artificial tasting white chocolate cream.

The Périgord truffle dusted in cocoa, with a good strong cocoa aroma, was a crisp well-tempered chocolate filled with a whipped rum truffle.

A pink foil-wrapped liqueur chocolate could have been kirsch, raspberry, or blackberry. The dark chocolate was a little burnt and had a strong artificial vanilla aroma, and the liqueur filling itself was rather syrupy.

The walnut dark chocolate was a very good aromatic dark chocolate, not too strong or bitter; and the walnut gianduja: very hard and sweet.

A dark chocolate filled with a dense chalky white buttercream filling was very sweet, as was the praline truffle with its smooth texture.

The Dior truffle in a gold foil cup was milk chocolate with a filbert and had coffee flavor; while a milk chocolate jewel-shaped square had inside it a soft very alcoholic ganache that tasted of kirsch.

The white chocolate and roasted almond cup had good almonds, but the white chocolate was rather too sweet and crumbly in texture.

L. HEINER

CAFÉ KONDITOREI, 1010 VIENNA, WOLLZEILE 9, AUSTRIA
TEL: (43) 512 23 43

USEFUL INFORMATION:

STAR RATING: ★★

COUNTRY OF ORIGIN: *Austria*

AVAILABILITY: *From Café Konditorei in Wollzeilestraße, Vienna, Kärtner Straße 21-23, Vienna and 2380 Perchtoldsdorf, Wienergasse 16.*

BOX SIZES: *7 ounces and 8½ ounces.*

HOUSE SPECIALTIES: *Mozart Kugeln, nougat, truffles, Mandel Orange torte, and Prinz Eugen torte.*

COUVERTURES USED:

Top secret

La Praline Chocolatier

2A AVENIDA DE LOS PALOS GRANDES, EDIFICIO ARTELITO,
LOCAL 4, APTDO 2389, CARMELITAS, CARACAS, VENEZUELA
TEL: (58-2) 2 84 99 86   FAX: (58-2) 2 85 21 61

*T*he company was founded in 1985 by Belgian ex-patriots Ludo and Lisette Gillis, who finally settled in Venezuela after sojourns in Brazil and Argentina. Coming from a country with a tradition of producing handmade chocolates in every small village, Ludo Gillis was bowled over by the quality of Venezuelan cocoa. He hit upon the idea of learning how to make chocolates back home in Belgium, and he trained there with maître chocolatier Hans Burie in Antwerp for a year. This placement was hard won, and in a small country like Belgium where professional secrets are jealously guarded and normally kept strictly within the family, Ludo had to swear that he was not going to open up around the corner in competition. Gillis also took classes at the Piva school with famous professors such as Roger Geerts and F. Adriaenssens.

Thoroughly grounded in the skills of chocolate making, Ludo and Lisette Gillis returned to Caracas and set up their air-conditioned production unit. As Venezuela is located in the tropical zone, even winter daytime temperatures often average 70°F, which means that the locals have no preconceived ideas about chocolate seasons, they just love to eat it all year round! With locally grown fine criollo beans, which are so hard to come by in Europe, and fresh macadamia, cashew, and brazil nuts, a unique collection of tropical chocolates has evolved. The Venezuelan couverture manufacturer El Rey has collaborated with the Gillises to produce a premium-quality chocolate, using the rarest cocoa beans available and conching the chocolate for much longer than they had been accustomed to.

USEFUL INFORMATION:

STAR RATING: ★★
COUNTRY OF ORIGIN: *Venezuela*
AVAILABILITY: *From shops in Caracas, also 5-star hotels and outside caterers.*
BOX SIZES: *8 ounces, 1 pound, and 2¼ pounds.*
HOUSE SPECIALTIES: *Macadamia marzipan and cashew praline.*
COUVERTURES USED:
El Rey couverture made with rare Venezuelan cocoa beans in dark and milk chocolate, with a particularly fine and mild aroma. White couverture imported from Belcolade in Belgium.

TASTING NOTES:

This was a classic Belgian assortment of well-crafted molded chocolates. As fresh cream is used, they must be eaten very quickly (some of the samples were already moldy). When I visited the factory in Caracas, they tasted very different and much better than the previous samples.

The Maiz (corn on the cob) chocolate mousse was very fluffy with a sweet filling. Heart was a Cointreau ganache in dark chocolate, and Vanessa a praline.

Macadamia marzipan was definitely the most interesting and successful chocolate, incorporating chunks of macadamia.

Four others tasted were Cupid, a very buttery caramel with slightly burned taste; Tree Trunk, a good, slightly crunchy croquant; Caribe-Moka, that was not too sweet and very good; and Marzipan which had a good grainy texture of fresh ground nuts, but was too sweet.

1 pound gift box from La Praline.

$\mathscr{L}$ALONDE

his house was founded in 1850 by Jean-Frederic Goddefroy Lillig, and from the outset the business was centered on both confectionery and chocolates. With his nephew, Monsieur Lillig invented the Bergamot, which has become a typical specialty of the Alsace region, to the point that Bergamots de Nancy is now the commonly used name for these flat square sugar candies flavored with bergamot oil. In 1901 Albert Lalonde took over the business, and the family ran the house until 1970, when it was bought by Fernand Bader. He was joined in 1984 by Jean-Luc Guillevic, who has been running the business since 1994. All the chocolatiers working at Lalonde are trained in-house and customarily stay loyal to their maître until they retire. The recipes, techniques, and trade secrets that have developed over more than a hundred and fifty years are thus in safe hands and form an integral part of the business.

Today, in addition to the Bergamots, the confectionery business is based on craquelines; nine types of sweetmeat, each with a marzipan base, flavored with a different fruit or alcohol, and encased in a thin layer of caramelized sugar; and the Duchesses de Lorraine, which are almond or filbert pralines encased in royal icing. Quite apart from these sugar confections, Lalonde also makes some of the best artisan chocolates in France.

USEFUL INFORMATION:

STAR RATING: ★ ★
COUNTRY OF ORIGIN: *France*
AVAILABILITY: *From two shops in Nancy and Metz, worldwide mail-order catalog.*
BOX SIZES: *8 ounces, 12 ounces, 1 pound, 1½ pounds, and 2 pounds, also gift boxes.*
HOUSE SPECIALTIES: *Pralitas—an almond praline croquante; Pavé du Roi—an almond praline with pistachio; Nelusco—a hazelnut praline flavored with coffee; Stanislas —a pear ganache; Feuillantines—a grape ganache. Chocolate liqueurs filled with raspberry, mirabelle plum, and kirsch eau de vie; the Chardons de Lorraine which look like hand-dipped truffles filled with similar liqueurs.*
COUVERTURES USED:
Mainly Valrhona's Caraque and Extra bitter for dark chocolate; superalpina for milk chocolate.

TASTING NOTES:

Robust 1950s style packaging, reminiscent of macho aftershave boxes, had ensured successful transit of the chocolates and preserved the strong fragrance of fine dark chocolate.

There are over sixty varieties of chocolate which come in three basic types: almond and filbert pralines; ganaches and truffles; and chocolate liqueurs.

The chocolates were presented in glossy, shiny lines, all hand-dipped except for one in the shape of a leaf and a dark chocolate palet with a cocoa butter transfer of a crown and the Lalonde name, containing a crunchy praline.

The palet d'or was faultless, its ganache full of fruit, body, and delicately flavored vanilla, with a smooth melting texture.

There was also a subtly flavoured Grand Marnier ganache, dipped in dark chocolate and perfectly tempered; an unusually delicate cherry preserved in brandy inside a chocolate dome and wrapped in red foil.

$\mathscr{L}$E $\mathscr{C}$HOCOLATIER

1834 NE 164TH STREET, NORTH MIAMI BEACH,
FLORIDA 36162
TEL: (305) 944-3020   FAX: (305) 354-8489

$\mathscr{S}$tarted in 1980 by Nancy Jehlen as a hobby and small business, Le Chocolatier soon developed a reputation for quality and excellence, and won many awards for its chocolates. In 1986, Joseph Marmor and Baruch Schaked bought the shop and more than tripled the volume of chocolates produced. The company supplies major hotels, cruise lines, caterers, and gourmet stores throughout south Florida.

The maître chocolatier is Baruch Schaked, who studied chocolate making in Germany and also ran one of the major chocolate factories in Argentina.

STAR RATING: ★

COUNTRY OF ORIGIN: *United States*

AVAILABILITY: *Mail order anywhere in the U.S.*

BOX SIZES: *Ballotins—2 or 4 piece; boxes 4 ounces, 8 ounces, 12 ounces, 1 pound, 1½ pounds, and 2 pounds.*

HOUSE SPECIALTIES: *Four truffles: plain, amaretto, Grand Marnier, and fresh raspberry. Many festive holiday ideas, and a kosher range of chocolates. Various sizes of chocolate bottle, Stars of David, clogs, sleighs, swans, hearts, chocolate platters, and baskets.*

COUVERTURES USED:

Guittard, an American company started in 1868.

TASTING NOTES:

The truffles were quite good and straightforward, although they looked rather odd with colored sugar coverings to differentiate the various tastes. Interesting lichen-like patterns of cocoa powder and powdered sugar dusted the square shapes. All in all, the fondants were too sweet and had some strange flavor experiments.

There was a very good dark ganache with a soft and pleasant texture and good dark chocolate; a rum ganache that was very buttery and smooth in which the alcohol was not too strong but just right; and a good, plain, well-made square truffle. Others, less well liked, were a round, dark vanilla fondant with white stripes that was very sweet and had too solid a vanilla filling that was not good; and the maple fondant which, though it had good fragrance, was too sweet.

The milk chocolate-covered Amaretto Marzipan—more successful than the fondants— stuck to the teeth nevertheless. Though it had a good aroma, it was also too sweet. It contained ground amaretto biscuits, orange peel, and perhaps some orange juice.

The spearmint filling of the Lemon Pie— bright yellow with chalky white cover—was very sticky with an artificial-tasting tang. It was the least-liked chocolate in the box.

Le Chocolatier
FINE CHOCOLATE

L E ROUX

18 RUE DU PORT-MARIA, 56170 QUIBERON, FRANCE
TEL: (33) 97 50 06 83   FAX: (33) 97 30 57 94

*L*e Roux Caramelier-Chocolatier was founded in 1977 in the spa and seaside resort of Quiberon by Henri Le Roux and his wife Lorraine. Originally the shop sold ice-cream and chocolate, but the success of the chocolates soon took over, making the ice-cream redundant. Le Roux has achieved national and international success, partly by the creation of the famous, and much-imitated, Caramel au Beurre Salé. As outstanding as the caramel, the chocolates are also exquisitely made in the best of French traditions—very rich in chocolate and butter, not sweet, and extremely delicate—while their technical virtuosity may owe much to the Swiss tradition.

Henri Le Roux, the maître chocolatier, is the son of a pâtissier who worked in the U.S., Australia, and France, where Henri was exposed to the world of pastry and chocolate from his tender years. After a rigorous apprenticeship in the Swiss tradition, Le Roux returned to his place of birth, Pont l'Abbé, where he rounded off his education, carrying on the secrets that his father had left behind, before starting his own enterprise with his wife in 1977. He has proved to be one of the great innovators with his Caramel au Beurre Salé (salted butter caramel), his Petites Douceurs Gourmandes ("little sweetmeats"), and other original recipes that seem to owe their flavor mainly to the French tradition.

Le Roux's chocolates are available in numerous sizes and styles of boxes.

USEFUL INFORMATION:

STAR RATING: ★ ★ ★

COUNTRY OF ORIGIN: *France*

AVAILABILITY: *From the shop in Quiberon and worldwide mail-order.*

BOX SIZES: *Numerous*

HOUSE SPECIALTIES: *Henri Le Roux and truffle king Jacques Pebeyre collaborated in 1989 to create a smooth dark chocolate truffle, with small pieces of fresh black Périgord truffle, which won two Coq d'Or awards. I did not have an opportunity to taste this creation, but apparently it is an exquisite combination, with the delicate perfume of the truffle coming through. It is available during the truffle season, October to February.*

COUVERTURES USED: *French-made*

TASTING NOTES:

CORTÉS: *Aromatic and melting, this was a rich chocolatey ganache on a foundation of almond praline.*

CBS: *The chewy caramel with a salty tang, which comes from the salted butter, was an outstandingly successful combination of sweet and salt with the addition of crunchy almonds and hazelnuts.*

KYRA: *A very delicate coffee ganache, Kyra had a slightly grainy texture, and a little Cognac.*

SUZETTE: *This crunchy walnut praline was rather sweet.*

SYLVIE: *The plain ganache was very smoothly bitter and was a melting combination.*

The selection also included Louison, a caramel made with fruit and enrobed in the finest layer of chocolate; Tantzor, a ganache made from pure criollo beans, seated on a layer of ginger marzipan; and Harem, a ganache made with mint tea, inspired by the freshness of an oasis, we are told.

ℒETUFFE

10 PLACE FRANCOIS, LOUVEL, ANGOULEME, FRANCE
TEL: (33) 45 95 00 54

The business that had been founded in 1873 was bought by the Letuffe family in 1950. They produced traditional artisan chocolates and in 1955 introduced new technology, by way of an enrobing machine. When the current director, Jean-Pierre Letuffe, took over the business, production focused on regional traditions and drew inspiration from their own regional ingredients, using the beurre de Charentes and crème fraîche.

Making pralines at Letuffe.

USEFUL INFORMATION:

STAR RATING: ★ ★

COUNTRY OF ORIGIN: *France*

AVAILABILITY: *From the shop in Angoulême and a mail-order catalog.*

BOX SIZES: *8 ounces, 12 ounces, 1 pound, 1½ pounds, 2¼ pounds, and 3 pounds. Also luxury gift boxes 1¼ pounds, 1¼ pounds, and 2¼ pounds.*

HOUSE SPECIALTIES: *Palets d'Or; Salamandres, a chocolate cream flavored with raisins and milk caramel, derived from the coat of arms of Francois I; Cognaçais, a chocolate depicting the coat of arms of the town of Cognac; Marguerite d'Angoulême which was created as a tribute to Marguerite de Valois, sister of Francois I. Other chocolates are made with the local cream, butter, and alcohol.*

COUVERTURES USED:

Top secret

TASTING NOTES:

The opened box, beautifully wrapped and presented in crisp, white pleated paper, revealed a rather incongruous modern glossy black and red ballotin inside, and the smell of orange that pervaded the whole box was a little overwhelming. The creamy, buttery, Charentais tradition came through very strongly, but the chocolate itself tasted rather bland, with vanilla and orange flavors predominating.

The milk chocolate tulip was very sweet, and the chocolate made with vanilla and almond essence, which had a violet petal on top, contained a ganache flavored with licorice.

Generally the alcohol was overpowering. Chocolat au Pineau de Charentes, a dark chocolate shell with a sugar crust, had very strong alcohol inside, and there were several chocolates that were filled with a fiery eau de vie, possibly Pineau de Charentes, which was almost too strong, and some of the nutty chocolates were a bit soggy, making it difficult to decide whether they were almond or pistachio

$\mathcal{M}$ARY

73 RUE ROYAL, 1000 BRUSSELS, BELGIUM
TEL: (32-2) 217 45 00

$\mathcal{M}$arie Delluc founded the chocolaterie-confiseur Mary, in 1919. She was appointed the first chocolate supplier to the Belgian Royal Household in 1942, and the warrant was subsequently renewed in 1990 and 1994. The business has remained in the family's hands and is currently owned by the third generation.

The maître chocolatier is Jean Lamberty, who fulfilled his childhood dream of becoming a chocolate maker when he married into the family. These chocolates are a must for anyone who loves very rich, creamy, and buttery fillings. The chocolates are wrapped in gold foil, which is unusual for fine chocolate, as it hides their gloss and the skill which went into their creation. They are mostly molded into simples shapes, quite large and well crafted. The buttery ganache is not overly sweet, as is so often the case with Belgian chocolates.

Classical interior of the shop in Brussels.

STAR RATING: ★

COUNTRY OF ORIGIN: *Belgium*

AVAILABILITY: *From the shop in Brussels—retail sales only!*

BOX SIZES: *8 ounces, 1 pound, 1½ pounds, and 2¼ pounds.*

HOUSE SPECIALTIES: *Pralines enrobed with very dark chocolate, containing at least 70 to 90 percent cocoa solids that balance the sweet buttery centers, often made with crème fraîche. The line consists of 72 different varieties, mainly molded chocolate cups with a mixture of praline, croquant, and buttercream filling. They are all handmade and no artificial coloring or flavorings are used. Seasonal specialties are clogs for the feast of St. Nicholas, Christmas logs, nativity scenes modeled from marzipan, and Easter eggs.*

COUVERTURES USED: *Specially made by Callebaut from their choice of 440 blended beans couvertures.*

TASTING NOTES:

A cup with a lid of almond brittle was overly sweet, and the praline inside was dotted with more of the croquant. Second dark chocolate cup with a milk lid housed a very runny brandy buttercream, colored with chocolate.

The milk chocolate basket was full of coffee buttercream, with finely chopped almonds to add texture to a rich and sweet center.

The dark ice cube shape contained buttercream filling resembling cake icing, and black specks of Bourbon vanilla. But alas, it was too sweet.

There was also a cherry soaked in brandy and surrounded by dark ganache; an almond-shaped milk chocolate with a caramelly ganache which was good and well balanced; and the "Mary," a square chocolate, dark and very crunchy.

ℳELCHIOR ℭHOCOLATES

STATION ROAD, SOUTH MOLTON, DEVON EX36 3LL, UK
TEL: (44-1769) 574442

*I*n 1977 Swiss-born Carlo Melchior opened a seaside restaurant in the West Country with his English wife. Unable to find any really good-quality chocolates to serve with the coffee after dinner, Carlo, with a strong vision and conviction about chocolate, decided to try his own hand. Remembering what Swiss chocolates tasted like, Melchior quickly realized that he was capable of producing something very similar himself. For the first few years, these chocolates were to be the rare privilege of the restaurant clientele, until he was so encouraged by the feedback that he took the radical step of selling the restaurant, and relocating to the small Devonshire village of Chittlehampton. There, the Melchiors bought a property with outbuildings and soon converted them into a kitchen and chocolate workshop. Before marketing the chocolates,

Carlo Melchior attended a number of courses in Switzerland, and only when he was totally happy with his product did he visit potential clients. The first was Fortnum & Mason in London, whose response was very positive; the store is now one of Melchior's best customers, even developing a line of specialty chocolates with them. Since then Melchior has expanded its market to include a number of specialist outlets throughout Britain. After winning Henrietta Green's rosette for Best Chocolates in Britain in 1993, a move to larger premises is planned in 1995.

Selection of the many seasonal specialties available.

USEFUL INFORMATION:

STAR RATING: ★★
COUNTRY OF ORIGIN: *Britain*
AVAILABILITY: *Fortnum & Mason, Mangetout in Guernsey, and other outlets. Worldwide mail order.*
BOX SIZES: *From 12 ounces to 4½ pounds.*
HOUSE SPECIALTIES: *Fruit and liqueur truffles; liquid center liqueur chocolates; personalized chocolate logos; and Christmas novelties.*
COUVERTURES USED: *Max Felchlin, Maestrani.*

TASTING NOTES:

These are beautiful, skillfully made classic Swiss-style chocolates. The dark truffles were rich, smooth, and alcoholic: excellent milk champagne, kirsch, and framboise. Some combinations of strawberry and banana with white chocolate might not find favor with French purists, but no doubt have their aficionados.

MICHEL CHAUDUN

149 RUE DE L'UNIVERSITÉ, 75007 PARIS, FRANCE
TEL: (33-1) 47 53 74 40

*H*aving opened his own shop in 1986, itself a masterpiece of order and harmony, Michel Chaudun is often to be seen behind the counter, welcoming locals and celebrities with equal warmth. When he's hard at work in the laboratory behind the shop, his wife takes charge in the shop.

Chaudun started his apprenticeship some thirty years ago, at the age of 14. He trained as a chocolatier, glacier, and pâtissier, then arrived in Paris where he worked in all the best chocolate houses, notably Robert Linxe's La Maison de Chocolat, and Maison LeNôtre. He also traveled abroad, working with Swiss chocolatier Withmer. He specializes not only in making some of the finest chocolates in the world, but also creates the most unbelievable sculptures

Lavishly packaged chocolates
including a wax-sealed "cigarette box."

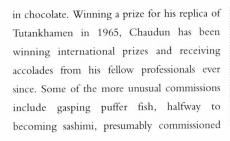

in chocolate. Winning a prize for his replica of Tutankhamen in 1965, Chaudun has been winning international prizes and receiving accolades from his fellow professionals ever since. Some of the more unusual commissions include gasping puffer fish, halfway to becoming sashimi, presumably commissioned by a Japanese client, and a pair of false teeth which would look perfectly at home on a Halloween candy counter.

Michel Chaudun remains faithful to his philosophy of "giving oneself pleasure and giving pleasure," and he says, "good chocolate is that which wakes people up with a 'choc'."

USEFUL INFORMATION:

STAR RATING: ★ ★ ★

COUNTRY OF ORIGIN: *France*

AVAILABILITY: *From shops in Paris and Tokyo.*

BOX SIZES: *8 ounces, 12 ounces, 1 pound. Chests 12 ounces to 6½ pounds. Small boxes 4 ounces and 8 ounces.*

COUVERTURES USED:

The best French couvertures enrobe all the chocolates; none are molded. The rare cocoas which make up these couvertures are: South American criollo and trinitario, *Venezuelan,* arriba *(Ecuador),* while African and Ivory Coast forasteros are used to give robustness and balance to the other fine beans.

Maître chocolatier Michel Chaudun.

TASTING NOTES:

In a beautiful box, opening like a cigarette box, were small squares of couverture with an exquisite bouquet and finish. Another box held tiny disks of bitter chocolate and toasted almonds, from a different blend of rare beans, that were elegant, smooth, round, and complex with a really good long finish.

From the whole range of 30 or so different chocolates, including subtly flavored ganaches and pralines, all hand-enrobed rather than dipped, each chocolate was perfection and became my benchmark of really fine quality.

Tastings included the palet d'or, *a very smooth ganache of rich chocolate flavor with a long finish;* Samurai, *a ganache with vanilla and praline;* Veragua, *a praline caramel that was very good, though rather sweet; and a dome-shaped dark chocolate with a white chocolate tip. This was a succulent rum-soaked raisin on a bed of almond paste, with a dark ganache on top. It was very good.*

A really delicious orangette was among the best I ever tasted. The orange rind had no pith and was very fine in texture, and the dark chocolate surrounding it was studded with toasted almonds—a sensational combination.

The dark chocolate disks had tiny fragments of crunchy roasted cocoa nib crushed into them, with a smooth couverture that was intense and that melted easily.

MICHELI

1 RUE MICHELI-DU-CREST, 1205 GENEVA, SWITZERLAND
TEL: (41-22) 329 90 06   FAX: (41-22) 781 40 34

Husband and wife team Pierre and Liliane Poncioni have devoted the last thirty years of their lives to this chocolate business. Pierre makes the chocolates, while Liliane runs the shop, and in spite of their long hours, both remain smiling—they just love their work. Their daughter Jannick and their son Didier are also involved in the business: Jannick makes the cakes for the little tea room, where in the summer you can also eat ice cream on the terrace, and Didier does all the paperwork.

Micheli should win a prize for being the only Swiss chocolatier to specialize in dark chocolate—not any old dark, but pure, unadulterated, 100 percent cocoa bars. Explaining his passion for dark chocolate, Pierre says, "To begin with everyone loves milk chocolate, then you change. It's like wine, Burgundy is what all the great wine lovers end up with."

TASTING NOTES:

DARK CHOCOLATE WITH AN
ALMOND: *Filled with a subtle delicately crunchy praline, this had a hint of orange.*

TRIANGULAR SHAPE IN DARK
CHOCOLATE: *It was filled with caramelized almonds and a milky praline, with a good lingering nutty flavor. It was very good, although a little difficult to eat, as it tended to fracture as it was bitten into!*

NOISETTE SANDWICH: *With orange on the outer layers, it was very sweet, slightly artificial-tasting, and gritty in texture, also the orange flavor had tainted its neighbors in the box.*

PIPED MILK CHOCOLATE: *This looked enticing, but concealed a glacé cherry – not my favorite combination, to be reserved for the very sweet-toothed!*

ROUND DARK CHOCOLATE BALL: *Filled with a very strongly alcoholic truffle and marzipan, the chocolate shell was beautifully crunchy, the ganache very smooth, and the marzipan quite grainy, an interesting combination of textures and flavors, dominated by the alcohol.*

RECTANGULAR DARK CHOCOLATE:
The crisp shell gave way to a sweet praline, full of freshly toasted nuts, well balanced by the very bitter chocolate on the outside, with a good long finish.

The 100 percent Brazilian cocoa bar did not have a very distinctive aroma and was slow to melt in the mouth. It was an interesting experience, though, and perfect with a cup of really bitter espresso coffee.

USEFUL INFORMATION:

STAR RATING: ★ ★
COUNTRY OF ORIGIN: *Switzerland*
AVAILABILITY: *From the shop in Geneva and worldwide mail-order.*
BOX SIZES: *numerous*
HOUSE SPECIALTIES: *75, 85, and even 100 percent cocoa chocolate bars; truffles; Pavé Genevois; ice cream; cakes and tea.*
COUVERTURES USED:
Top secret

OBERWEIS

19 GRAND-RUE – L-1661 LUXEMBOURG
TEL: (352) 47 07 03   FAX (352) 49 31 41

This confissier, pâtissier, and glacier has become one of the great institutions in Luxembourg. Founded in 1964 by Pit Oberweis, joined now by his two sons, the business has expanded to a point that they have had to relocate their production to a purpose-built unit. The latest venture also has a small restaurant, which seats 100 people and serves light meals. Oberweis now has 5 shops in the Grand Duchy, employing 90 staff, and it has been honored with membership of the prestigious Relais Desserts.

USEFUL INFORMATION:

STAR RATING: ★★
COUNTRY OF ORIGIN: *Belgium*
AVAILABILITY: *From 5 shops around Luxembourg. Worldwide mail order.*
BOX SIZES: *Numerous*
HOUSE SPECIALTIES: *Speculoos, Printen, Baseler, Leckerli, Spitzkuchen, Stollen, Bambkuch, and marzipan figures.*
COUVERTURES USED:
Valrhona for the ganache centers, Lindt for dipping and molded truffle shells.

ORTRUD MÜNCH CARSTENS

425 EAST 58TH STREET, NEW YORK, NEW YORK 10022
TEL: (212) 751-9591

Ortrud Carstens has carved a niche in the highly specialized chocolate market in New York since opening her business in 1987. She uses only the finest ingredients and couverture available, and everything is made with meticulous care. Where possible, fresh organic produce is used; unsweetened fruit purées and herb infusions. The tea used in the Earl Grey truffle comes from Marriage Frères in the rue Bourg-Tibourg in Paris's 4th arrondissement, in my opinion the best tea house in the world, and well worth a detour. The finest vanilla is shipped from Tahiti, fresh cinnamon sticks are used, and rare coffee beans freshly infused. The super-fresh chocolates are distributed daily through carefully chosen gourmet food retailers and selected caterers. Carstens' philosophy is to "create bonbons which are high in cocoa, and low in sugar, thus enabling you to experience the full flavor of the chocolate, with all its subtle floral, fruity herbal, or spicy nuances and overtones. No matter what type of chocolate bonbon, the inherent multidimensional character of the couverture is never overpowered by any added flavors: it is the graceful marriage of chocolate and the other natural ingredients of the highest order."

To balance her seriously purist attitude to chocolate, Ortrud Carstens also makes the most delightful whimsical creations, including "rusty" chocolate tools, needless to say out of the world's finest couverture. For her work she has picked up numerous citations including Best Chef in America in 1990, and she presents in-depth seminars on chocolate making for private clients, as well as to the popular and trade press. Other projects include commissions such as white chocolate calla lilies with stem ginger stamens, a hand-rolled chocolate cigar filled with champagne ganache made for a famous American couturier, and much other work commissioned by designers from Europe and the U.S.

Chocolate "rusty tools."

USEFUL INFORMATION:

STAR RATING: ★ ★ ★
COUNTRY OF ORIGIN: *United States*
AVAILABILITY: *From Dean & Deluca in New York and Washington DC; Mad 61, and Manhattan Fruiterer in New York.*
BOX SIZES: *Chocolates are sold in bulk or by the piece, and the tools are available as a set in a special wooden carpenters' tool box.*
HOUSE SPECIALTIES: *Truffles, palet, custom-molded and handcrafted artistic chocolate pieces, dipped fruit, and special molds for Thanksgiving, Christmas, Valentine's Day and other holidays.*
COUVERTURES USED: *Exclusively Valrhona, especially the Grand Cru ones made from rare bean varieties.*

TASTING NOTES:

Paper thin hand-cut slices of dried Bartlett pears from California's western shore orchards are half-dipped in an explosively fruity dark couverture, which harmonizes perfectly with the natural acidity and grainy texture of the fruit; an outstanding and original combination.

A perfect glossy round wafer of bitter chocolate forms a lily-pad for a strip of tangy orange peel, dried cranberry, or stem ginger. The Earl Grey truffles are masterful in their fragrance and delicacy—perfect harmony between chocolate, cream, and scented tea.

$\mathscr{P}$ALAIS DU $\mathscr{C}$HOCOLAT

1200 19TH STREET, NW, WASHINGTON DC 20036
TEL: (202) 659-4244

With his high-quality French chocolates and patisseries, maître chocolatier Dominique Leborgne at Palais de Chocolat quickly established a niche market. He has a wholesale production unit in Tacoma Park, Maryland, which supplies among others the Ritz-Carlton and Jean-Louis at the Watergate.

Leborgne had a thorough and star-studded training in France, winning gold medals at the Grand Prix Internationale de la Chocolaterie in France and at the World Gastronomic Exhibition in Frankfurt and numerous others. He has also trained at Dalloyau Gavillon and was head pastry chef at the Intercontinental in Paris, after which he was invited to Washington to open the Willard Intercontinental. He has brought in European chocolate technology and has one of only two German chocolate-coating conveyor belts in the U.S.

Importing only the finest chocolates from France and Belgium, Leborgne maintains his roots in the French tradition, visiting France several times a year to keep in touch with professional colleagues and new developments. He explains the different between mass-produced and artisan chocolate that whatever the time of year: "We make it day by day, but the big factories are already preparing for next Christmas."

On the inside are shiny and beautifully finished chocolates.

In the early days he would sometimes turn down orders, believing that slow, steady growth was preferable to risking a decline in quality: a perfectionist to the end.

USEFUL INFORMATION:

STAR RATING: ★ ★
COUNTRY OF ORIGIN: *United States*
AVAILABILITY: *From 3 locations in Washington DC. Mail-order catalog for delivery within U.S.*
BOX SIZES: *2 pieces, 4 pieces, ballotins of 8 pieces, 16 pieces, and 30 pieces.*
HOUSE SPECIALTIES: *Those mentioned in Tasting Notes and seasonal specialties of molded figures and fruit paste.*
COUVERTURES USED:
Callebaut, Cacao Barry, and Valrhona's Guanaja and Caraque.

TASTING NOTES:

RASPBERRY: *A flat tombstone-like chocolate finished with cocoa encased a very subtle, smooth, almost liquid raspberry ganache.*

AMARETTO: *A very sweet milk chocolate ganache which had a good texture and delicate amaretto flavor.*

COFFEE: *The dark chocolate coffee ganache was smooth and buttery.*

VALENTIN: *A dark chocolate heart was filled with a smooth but rather bland caramel ganache.*

SCOTTISH TRUFFLE: *This chocolate log, dusted in powdered sugar, contained a milk truffle flavored with Scotch whiskey.*

WILD TRUFFLE: *A cocoa-dusted light fluffy truffle, this was very smooth and buttery, but lacking in chocolate.*

EARL GREY: *My favorite was an ex mely delicately perfumed, creamy and sweet, u !l-balanced tea ganache.*

PELTIER

66 RUE DE SÈVRES, 75007 PARIS, FRANCE
TEL: (33-1) 47 34 08 62   FAX: (33-1) 40 65 93 98

6 RUE SAINT-DOMENIQUE, 75007 PARIS, FRANCE
TEL: (33-1) 47 05 50 02

*P*eltier was founded in 1880 and quickly became famous for its sorbets. Peltier is a relative newcomer to the world of chocolate, starting its artisan chocolate production in 1978. This side of the business has grown and now employs three chocolatiers.

USEFUL INFORMATION:

STAR RATING: ★ ★

COUNTRY OF ORIGIN: *France*

AVAILABILITY: *From the two shops in Paris.*

BOX SIZES: *Ballotins plus a selection of jewel boxes and porcelain bowls filled with chocolates.*

HOUSE SPECIALTIES: *Muscadine truffles, Sèvrelinettes, Lucien, special commissions accepted. Seasonal specialties include Father's Day pipes and tools, and masks and clowns for Carnival.*

COUVERTURES USED: *Valrhona and Cacao Barry.*

PIERRE COLAS

2 RUE CAMPAGNE, 4577 MODAVE, BELGIUM
TEL: (32-2) 648 08 93   FAX: (32-2) 41 21 76

ousins Quentin Michel and Laurent Michel started Pierre Colas in 1987 while they were university students in Liege and Brussels. They wanted a business they could run on a very small scale in parallel with their studies. Quentin Michel graduated in Political Science, with no previous experience of chocolate making, and his cousin Laurent Michel graduated in Business and Management Studies, but had worked as an apprentice pastry chef in Brussels, learning the rudiments of chocolate making at the same time.

The Michel's chocolate expertise has been learned by trial and error while developing the Pierre Colas brand. The nerve center and kitchen is in a tiny farmhouse in the middle of the countryside, where the chocolate is tempered on marble slabs, and the antique molds are individually filled by hand. Theirs is a very labor-intensive business, and a truly artisan production.

USEFUL INFORMATION:

STAR RATING: ★★

COUNTRY OF ORIGIN: *Belgium*

AVAILABILITY: *From specialist chocolate retailers in Belgium, Spain, and France. Exclusive to Rococo in London—a list of outlets is available from them.*

BOX SIZES: *2¼ ounce bar or 20 bar sampler box.*

HOUSE SPECIALTIES: *2¼ ounce chocolate bars.*

COUVERTURES USED:

Made by Belcolade, an excellent small Belgian producer.

TASTING NOTES:

The 12 ounce chocolate bars were composed of unusual combinations of dark and milk chocolate with herbs and spices, as well as a repertoire of more classic combinations. The esoteric combinations of pink peppercorns, thyme, lavender, cardamom, juniper, and Earl Grey tea work unexpectedly well, the robustness of the dark chocolate (60 percent cocoa mass), balancing perfectly these volatile combinations. Other bars include coffee, nougatine, grilled almonds, coconut, cinnamon, crystallized stem ginger, orange peel, and caramel.

PIERRE GINET

9 RUE DE LA CHARITÉ, 69002 LYON, FRANCE
TEL: (33) 78 42 09 82   FAX: (33) 78 37 94 07

Pierre Ginet, artisan maître chocolatier, who started his company in 1965, prides himself on his rigorous selection of raw materials and their quality, and his company's service to its customers. The company produces "haute couture" chocolates and has won various prizes at French and European chocolate fairs.

This prize-winning quality was certainly evident in the beautifully presented, glossy rows of chocolates, and the rich intense chocolate aroma on opening the box.

USEFUL INFORMATION:

STAR RATING: ★★

COUNTRY OF ORIGIN: *France*

AVAILABILITY: *From the shop in Lyon. Worldwide mail order.*

BOX SIZES: *8 ounces, 12 ounces, 1 pound, 1¼ pounds, 2¼ pounds, and 3½ pounds.*

HOUSE SPECIALTIES: *Perle noir (black pearl), guignolos de Lyon, foulards de Lyon (Lyonnais scarves), palets d'or, truffes fleuries.*

COUVERTURES USED: *Valrhona*

$\mathcal{R}$ICHARD $\mathcal{D}$ONNELLY
$\mathcal{F}$INE $\mathcal{C}$HOCOLATES

1509 MISSION STREET, SANTA CRUZ, CALIFORNIA 95060,
TEL: (408) 458-4214

With the idea of selling by mail order only, the business was founded in 1988, but this was very seasonal, and soon the retail and wholesale side of the business was expanded. After following in his father's footsteps and studying law for a year at Ripon College, Wisconsin, Richard Donnelly soon realized that this was not the path he wished to tread. He moved to Europe to begin his chocolate-making career by studying for nearly 5 months at La Varenne's school in Paris, becoming an apprentice there and finishing his studies with the crowning glory of being accepted as an apprentice by Wittamer in Brussels.

Richard Donnelly's famous bite-sized bars of chocolate.

On returning to the U.S., Donnelly spent a season as chocolate maker and assistant pastry chef with Jean-Yves Duperret at the Nouvelle Pâtisserie in San Francisco. Although he had a thorough grounding in chocolate making in Europe, it was Duperret who really caught Donnelly's imagination, making cakes which surpassed even the finest in Europe. So, fired with enthusiasm, Donnelly had the idea of running a chocolate company. It operated from his mother's kitchen in Boston, eventually moving west to Santa Cruz, and Richard Donnelly is now one of the bright young American chocolatiers to watch out for!

Donnelly is famous for his bite-sized bars of chocolate that have a most sophisticated wrapping and an exciting array of flavors. Each bar is wrapped in one of a number of Japanese inspired handmade papers, in the earthy colors of light green, brown, gray, burgundy, or black. The size of the bar (12 ounces) is perfect—just enough to share with a few discerning friends. The bars look beautifully smooth and shiny. Donnelly coats the inside of the mold with a fine layer of chocolate, after which, the mixture is poured in; because of the fine outside layer, the integrity of the filling is retained, and there are no telltale bits sticking through the bar.

USEFUL INFORMATION:

STAR RATING: ★ ★ ★

COUNTRY OF ORIGIN: *United States*

AVAILABILITY: *Bars available from some coffee shops, mail-order catalog.*

BOX SIZES: *6 ounces, 12 ounces, and 1 pound.*

HOUSE SPECIALTIES: *Donnelly also stocks fine couverture from Callebaut and Valrhona that can be used for eating, baking or chocolate making. Seasonal specialties are chocolate wine bottles, filled with either an assortment of truffles or chocolate almonds.*

COUVERTURES USED:

Valrhona, Callebaut, and Cacao Barry.

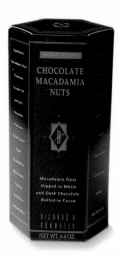

TASTING NOTES:

CHOCOLATE-DIPPED AUSTRALIAN APRICOT: *Turtle-shaped and sticky when unwrapped, the chocolate smelled very good and contained a very large, rather sweet, and moist apricot.*

DARK CHOCOLATE FILBERT: *This very crunchy, very good fruity chocolate had well-roasted filberts and was very fresh and beautifully made.*

COFFEE BUTTERCREAM: *The milk chocolate was not too sweet, and European in taste. It contained a fluffy and firm mousse.*

WHITE CHOCOLATE MACADAMIA NUT: *This was a very fine white chocolate compared to the excessive sweetness usually found.*

PISTACHIO MARZIPAN: *Refreshing in its absence of artificial flavors, this marzipan was very soft, moist, and light.*

FILBERT GIANDUJA: *The lozenge-shaped milk chocolate had dense but soft ganache with tiny pieces of freshly ground mild coffee. The slight bitterness balanced well with the milk, and both tastes blended very well as the truffle quickly melted in the mouth—perfect consistency, too!*

CHOCOLATE TRUFFLES: *These properly handmade truffles with their elongated, uneven shapes wrapped in foil, were covered with fragrant cocoa powder.*

DOUBLE-DIPPED MACADAMIA NUT: *The Macadamias had been first dipped in white and then in plain chocolate that combined excellently with a slightly salty nut. It had a good, bitter aftertaste, and the nuts had a firm but soft texture which made it very agreeable to bite into.*

ROCOCO

BY NIGEL SLATER

321 KINGS ROAD, LONDON SW3 5EP, UK
TEL: (44-171) 352 5857   FAX: (44-171) 352 7360

*I*f you walk west along London's Kings Road, you will eventually come to Rococo. Designed and run by art-school graduate Chantal Coady, this small shop, decorated in candied-almond colors and piled high with beribboned bags and boxes, is one of Europe's most original and delightful shops.

Founded in 1983, Rococo is an Aladdin's cave of edible delights and has a gaiety about it that is far from the hallowed chocolate department of Harrods where Chantal Coady first worked as a student. I was transfixed by the shop's startling theatrical decoration, its magical atmosphere and its wonderful confections, but best of all there is chocolate. Rococo specializes in handmade artisan bars, made exclusively for the shop in a Belgian farmhouse kitchen. These

The engravings on Rococo's wrappers are from L'Etang's 1906 chocolate mold catalog.

USEFUL INFORMATION:

STAR RATING: ★★
COUNTRY OF ORIGIN: *Britain*
AVAILABILITY: *A limited selection available year round in The Conran Shop, London. Mail order.*
BOX SIZES: *8 ounces, 12 ounces, 1 pound, 1½ pounds, 2 pounds and huge 8 pound hatboxes.*
HOUSE SPECIALTIES: *Artisan and Grand Cru bars. In summer, physalis dipped in Caraïbe and strawberries in white chocolate; at Easter there are Grand Cru rabbits and quail, and eggs filled with different chocolates.*
COUVERTURES USED:
Valrhona, truffles made from Manjari, also Caraïbe for dipping.

TASTING NOTES:

The traditional English hand-dipped chocolates were filled with geranium, raspberry or coffee cream, pistachio marzipan, or dipped apricots and pears.

Rococo's fresh cream truffles ranged from dark chocolate-covered orange to Irish coffee and amaretto.

There were also its famous handmade "Truffes Maison" made from Valrhona's Manjari.

beautifully molded bars are flavored with startling originality, and the successful combination of the finest chocolate and original, even surprising, ingredients somehow sums up Chantal Coady's approach.

Rococo's Grand Cru bars are made from the world's finest cocoa beans and include Manjari, a magnificently fruity chocolate made from the criollo bean, a single bean chocolate with distinctive notes of balsam, almonds, and green tea. Rococo's House Bars include a very pure Chocolate Blanc and Amer, a rugged, slightly bitter chocolate. All are wrapped in silver or gold foil and the shop's distinctive blue and white wrapping paper.

$\mathcal{S}$ARA $\mathcal{J}$AYNE

517 OLD YORK ROAD, LONDON SW18 1TF, UK
TEL: (44-181) 874 8500

$\mathcal{S}$ara Jayne's love of chocolate and fine food began when she was at a convent school in North London, where the school lunches left much to be desired. In happy contrast, suppers cooked by her mother were inspired occasions and always of exceptional quality. After working for fifteen years as a film and TV commercial producer, Jayne underwent a "road to Damascus experience" in 1982, which led her to change careers and gave her the opportunity to indulge her latent passion for food and cooking. As Public Relations and Marketing Director of the Academie Culinaire de France based in Britain, she was surrounded by many of the country's greatest Academiciens: Albert and Michel Roux, the 3-star Michelin chefs; John Huber, senior lecturer at Thames Valley University; and Ian Ironside, head Pastry Chef at Gleneagles Hotel. Here Sara not only found inspiration, but was also able to learn at first hand from the experts, who gave their help and advice unstintingly.

Having perfected the art of chocolate making, Sara Jayne set up production in her kitchen at home, and these days she still works by day at the Academie Culinaire and by night she makes her renowned truffles. Using only chocolate, cream, and alcohol where demanded, her recipe does not include butter or any other fat; it is Jayne's opinion that anything other than cream makes the truffles undesirably heavy and cloying. "Butter and other fats are seriously inferior in flavor and have no real keeping advantage either. I have had fresh cream truffles tested in a laboratory, and they were just as good as those a week old." Ultimately, this is a matter of individual taste, as is the choice of couverture used. Sara Jayne hand-dips all her truffles, a task which she says has taken its toll after twelve years, for she now suffers from a unique self-inflicted injury: "truffle elbow."

Sara Jane's packaging
is as sophisticated as her chocolates.

USEFUL INFORMATION:

STAR RATING: ★★
COUNTRY OF ORIGIN: *Britain*
AVAILABILITY: *Specialties from St. Quentin, House of Albert Roux, and J. Sainsbury plc in London. Mail order.*
BOX SIZES: *8 ounces and 1 pound.*
HOUSE SPECIALTIES: *Made to order.*
COUVERTURES USED:
Cacao Barry 60 and 70 percent, including Ultime, and Fleur de Coa

TASTING NOTES:

The truffles were deliciously light and airy, the fillings pale in color, and the finish of each truffle quite distinct, although the textures were identical, and flavors of the line as a whole were not very distinct.

A bitter dark ganache was coated with dark chocolate; another dark ganache, with Calvados and blackberry, was dipped in dark chocolate and dusted with powdered sugar.

An ivory ganache log was flavored with Earl Grey tea; a Venus nipple, resembling a reverse-color Mont Blanc, of white chocolate topped with dark, was filled with a coffee ganache made from Arabica coffee and coffee liqueur.

A Champagne ganache made from "fine de Champagne" cognac was coated in white chocolate; there was a milk chocolate one; and finally a cocoa-dusted truffle filled with a delicate slightly crunchy ginger and spice, which was my favorite.

$\mathscr{S}$CHAETJENS

21 RUE DES 3 CAILLOUX, 80000 AMIENS, FRANCE
TEL: (33) 22 91 32 73   FAX: (33) 22 92 26 18

The Lenne family has runs its chocolate house for three generations now, and the site of the business has been occupied by professional confectioners since 1767. There are currently 14 employees in addition to Monsieur Lenne, the maître choco-latier, who has been a chocolatier since 1957, and his wife who joined him in 1965 to help with the running of the business.

Gift box from Schaetjens.

USEFUL INFORMATION:

STAR RATING: ★ ★

COUNTRY OF ORIGIN: *France*

AVAILABILITY: *From the shop in Amiens.*

BOX SIZES: *8 ounces to 2¼ pounds. Gift boxes: 12 ounces to 4½ pounds.*

HOUSE SPECIALTIES: *The Millennium Angel which has been created in homage to Amiens cathedral; the Saleika, a creation of Monsieur Lenne, this is a cherry soaked in fine champagne brandy for one year prior to being dipped in chocolate; pralines, both filbert and almond. A wide variety of Christmas specialties; and at Easter, handmade praline eggs made to order on the premises, which is unusual in that most chocolatiers buy their eggs from factories—the taste cannot be compared.*

COUVERTURES USED:

Valrhona's extra bitter, Café Noir, and the milk Superalpina. Cacao Barry's extra bitter Guyaquil, and Mi-amère. Mainly dark chocolate is used, with relatively little milk chocolate. All chocolates are hand-dipped.

TASTING NOTES:

A rectangular dark chocolate with three dark lines was an extremely good sweet praline; a round dark chocolate with a piece of peel on top had inside it a very sweet orange almond marzipan; and a round dark chocolate with two stripes on top had inside it an excellent dark whipped ganache.

A cherry in brandy—no stalk but a stone, so beware—had extremely potent alcohol.

There was a milk chocolate with a walnut on top, inside a walnut marzipan, though personally I would have preferred dark chocolate to balance the walnut.

$\mathscr{S}$LITTI

VIA FRANCESCA SUD, 240 51015 MONSUMMANO TERME
(PT), ITALY   TEL/FAX:(39-572) 640240

*A*ndrea Slitti's father opened the coffee-roasting house Caffè Slitti in 1969, but his young son, while delivering coffee to customers, who were mainly coffee shops and confectioners, became fascinated by chocolate. In 1986 the roasting house was re-located to much larger premises, and a coffee shop was added. Finding himself with extra space, Andrea Slitti took the opportunity to create his own chocolate workshop.

Although Slitti received some formal training in chocolate making, he refers to himself as a self-taught man, practically all of his knowledge having been acquired by spending whole days and nights in his workshop. Very quickly, he mastered the art of working in chocolate, and he started to create "wild and wonderful" objects in chocolate. Word spread—articles appeared in the press, and gourmet food lovers soon began to arrive. Slitti has been much in demand as a teacher, but steadfastly refuses to leave his shop. However, he generously devotes ten days a year to pupils in his own workshop, where he shows the basics of working with chocolate and also teaches the history of cocoa and the different cocoa varieties available.

Mixed chocolate bonbons.

In October 1993, after much coercion by his contemporaries, Slitti was persuaded to take part in the International Show held in Laragne, France. He walked away with the gold medal, beating all 43 participants. This victory, which was the first time an Italian had won such a prize in France, gave him the right to take part in the final of the Grand Prix International de la Chocolaterie, the biennial event held in Paris. Again, Slitti won the Grand Prix. for his artistic presentation, in competition with French, English, Spanish, American, and Japanese chocolatiers.

Maître chocolatier Andrea Slitti.

Rich chocolate spread.

USEFUL INFORMATION:

STAR RATING: ★ ★ ★

COUNTRY OF ORIGIN: *Italy*

AVAILABILITY: *From the shop in Monsummano Terme.*

BOX SIZES: *Numerous*

HOUSE SPECIALTIES: *"Rusty tools,"* *chocolate covered espresso beans and chocolate sculptures to order, including a chicken and a teapot.*

COUVERTURES USED:

Top secret

With charming, whimsical antique tools made from chocolate and "rusted" with cocoa powder, Slitti pushes the medium of chocolate to its limit with the masterpieces he makes, and he certainly stole the show at the Perugia Chocolate Festival in 1994. His chocolates are all visually stunning and the work of a fine craftsman.

TASTING NOTES:

The very ornate box, with gold poppy heads and made from recycled paper, held each chocolate individually cupped and gleaming.

The flavors were interesting and on the whole very subtle, but rather sweet—especially the milk chocolate snowman, a hazelnut-topped gianduja.

There was an excellent nut cluster with toasted rice crispies; and a beautiful burlap-imprinted oblong praline also with a bit of rice crispy.

The truffle was extraordinarily finely dipped. You could almost see the movement in the truffle, the precise moment of crystallization in the tempered chocolate. The slightly stiff truffle center was quite sweet and rum flavored.

A very good tea truffle with bits of dried tea finely sprinkled on top was on the sweet side.

The coffee, which reminded me of tiramisu, the Italian dessert, had a very strong, fresh, sweet coffee taste.

The milk chocolate square with its speckled-hen finish contained mandarin and Napoleon brandy; the Truffe d'or too much Chartreuse; and the milk square with almonds had an amaretto flavor which also was almost overpowering.

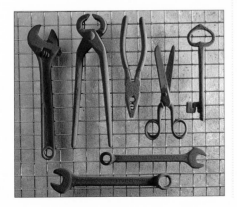

Chocolate "Rusty tools."

SPECIAL EDITION
CONTINENTAL CHOCOLATES

HONEYHOLES LANE, DUNHOLME, LINCOLNSHIRE
LN2 3SU, UK   TEL: [44-1673] 860616

pecial Edition literally translated from French slang means "village idiot," but there is nothing idiotic about the chocolate company launched in 1990 onto the UK market by Scotty Scott and Pam Andrews in Lincoln. One feature is the very dark chocolate with a minimum of 70 percent cocoa solids that they use, another is that only real brand-named alcohols are used, and never artificial flavoring or preservatives

Using the immediate environment as inspiration for their product line, Special Edition has created a Red Arrows chocolate bar under licence from and named for the daredevil Royal Air Force aerobatics team who are based nearby. Another novelty is a chocolate Lincoln imp, taken from the stone carving in the Cathedral.

Scotty Scott, the maître chocolatier, was born in Glasgow in 1935. During his six years of "tramping" around the world with the merchant navy, Scott became especially interested in international cuisine, something that was not much in evidence in Glasgow in those days! After leaving the merchant navy in 1959, Scott joined the RAF and spent the next 17 years flying Valiant and Vulcan bombers as an Electronics Officers.

Scott retired from the RAF in 1976 and turned his hand to a number of business ventures. In 1988, he met a couple, Mike and Pam Andrews who shared his passion for food, wine, and travel. Pam Andrews was in fact a professional caterer, so when the idea of a joint culinary venture was mooted, she joined Scott to form Special Edition.

USEFUL INFORMATION:
STAR RATING: ★
COUNTRY OF ORIGIN: *Britain*
AVAILABILITY: *Lincoln Cathedral shop, and in shops around Lincolnshire. Mail order.*
BOX SIZES: *8 ounces, 12 ounces, 1¼ pounds and 2 to 16 chocolate sizes.*
HOUSE SPECIALTIES: *Drunken Butterflies; Diamond Nine in milk chocolate; Red Arrow; Lincoln Imp; and after-dinner mints in dark and white chocolate.*
COUVERTURES USED:
Schokinag of Mannheim, and sometimes Maestrani white.

TASTING NOTES:

The milk chocolate is extremely pale in color. The selection is made almost entirely in molded shell in the Belgian tradition. The centers are well made, if on the sweet side.

DRUNKEN BUTTERFLY: *This milk chocolate with a Southern Comfort ganache was very smooth and good.*

CHOCOLATE BARREL: *A dark chocolate, this had rum-soaked raisins in a sweet liquid fondant.*

COATED SPLITTER TRUFFLE: *Roasted chopped pistachios (lots of them), almonds, and filberts in white chocolate and filbert praline were coated in milk chocolate—very sweet.*

GINGER WHIRL: *In bitter chocolate there was a sweet fondant with a strong ginger flavor and ginger pieces.*

APRICOT WHIRL: *In milk this chocolate was filled with a sweet apricot and condensed milk filling, reminiscent of cafeteria desserts.*

Another milk chocolate had a creamy sweet orange ganache and a subtle pistachio buttercream.

⒯RUFFLES

BROUGHAM HALL, BROUGHAM, PENRITH,
CUMBRIA CA10 2DE, UK
TEL: (44-1768) 867772

nce a fort, Brougham Hall, now home of The Old Smokehouse Truffles, stands on a site that has been both home and fort for centuries. In Victorian times, it became known as the "Windsor of the North," and was the home of the Lord Chancellor of England. Later visited by King Edward VII, but falling on hard times in the 1930s, the hall was rescued from dereliction in 1985 when it became a home for small craft industries, The Old Smokehouse chocolate makers among them in 1989. After two years, the chocolate business expanded to a retail unit in a new development in Penrith town center. Unfortunately, the recession took hold at the same time and after a disappointing year's trading, it closed down. Happily the truffle-making still prospers at Brougham Hall.

Classical Swiss truffles made in Britain.

Rona Newsom is the maître chocolatier who came into the profession after a career in journalism and publishing. She started The Old Smokehouse by smoking salmon, Cumberland hams, sausages, poultry, and cheeses—the smokery is still the mainstay of the business. When she branched out into chocolate making, she learned her skills from a Swiss chocolatier who gave her one-to-one tuition at Brougham Hall.

USEFUL INFORMATION:

STAR RATING: ★★

COUNTRY OF ORIGIN: *Britain*

AVAILABILITY: *From Brougham Hall and the Devonshire Arcade, Penrith. Mail-order catalog.*

BOX SIZES: *2 pieces, 7 ounces and 13 ounces.*

COUVERTURES USED:

Cacao Barry Mi-amère, Lactée Superior, Blanc Satin. There are plans to use Valrhona couverture in the future.

TASTING NOTES:

These classic Swiss truffles had some brave and interesting combinations. Made in pre-molded shells, the filled truffles are dipped into dark, milk, or white chocolate and finished with different kinds of sugar and vermicelli. The most remarkable were the apricot and pear varieties, which managed to combine the natural acidity of the fruit with the smooth richness of the chocolate and an extra kick from the eau-de-vie. The orange and ginger truffles were very good. Also popular, particularly with the more sweet-toothed, was the white Jamaican rum truffle dipped in toasted coconut.

WITTAMER

12 PLACE DU GRAND SABLON, GROTE ZAVEL 12,
1000 BRUSSELS, BELGIUM
TEL: (32-2) 512 84 51   FAX: (32-2) 512 37 42

Without a doubt the finest chocolate-makers in Belgium, Wittamer is another family dynasty akin to the Bernachons in Lyon, except that the chocolate-making side of the business was introduced only relatively recently by the grandson of the master baker Henri Wittamer who founded the enterprise in 1910. Born in Arlon, Belgium, of Austrian parents, he chose to set up his bakery in the Place du Grand Sablon in Brussels. He must have been a man of great vision because his quarter has become one of the chic shopping areas in Brussels and now is the center of the antiques trade. The business has expanded over the years and now owns several shops side by side, with different specialties: the bakery and pâtisserie, the chocolaterie, the icecreamery, the salon de thé, the traiteur and gourmet shop. Henri Wittamer's son, Henri-Gustave, is still involved in the management of the company, particularly with the bakery side, while his son

Henri Paul (known as Paul), the maître chocolatier, has expanded the ice cream and the pâtisserie areas, and was responsible for inaugurating the chocolate shop in 1988. In 1986 Henri Paul achieved the distinction of being made a member of the prestigious Relais Desserts, recently winning prizes for his Samba: a masterpiece of two contrasting chocolate mousses, and in Japan in 1989 his Akin (inspired by the Japanese word for autumn), which is a combination of chestnuts and chocolate. Paul's sister Myriam started the traiteur (outside catering) and gourmet service in 1985, and it has proved a huge success, especially among the international set based at the United Nations and European Union headquarters.

USEFUL INFORMATION:

STAR RATING: ★ ★ ★
COUNTRY OF ORIGIN: *Belgium*
AVAILABILITY: *From an outlet at Brussels airport. Worldwide mail order.*
BOX SIZES: *Mini ballotin; 10 ounces, 1 pound, 1½ pounds, and 2¼ pound ballotins.*
HOUSE SPECIALTIES: *A selection of over 60 varieties of praline, which include ganaches, giandujas, marzipans, truffles, fresh cream chocolates, orange and lemon peel dipped in chocolate, and nougatine. Seasonal specialties for St. Valentines, Secretary's Day, Mother's and Father's days, St. Nicholas, Christmas, and New Year, in fact any excuse to create new and exciting objects in chocolate. As Wittamer is a very small artisan business, it can readily respond to these very specialized feasts.*
COUVERTURES USED:
Made specially for Wittamer by Callebaut in Belgium.

TASTING NOTES:

PALET: *With its name printed in cocoa butter, this was a very fine ganache, rich in vanilla, butter, and cream with a good fragrant bouquet.*

DARK CHOCOLATE PYRAMID: *Again this had a very full fragrant aroma, lots of butter, and was not too sweet.*

WHITE TRUFFLE: *This was very white indeed. It had a dark center, but the white chocolate dominated.*

THÉ: *The chocolate with the red cocoa butter transfer had a very rich dark chocolate flavor which came through after a fragrant Earl Grey tea.*

MOLDED PARCEL WITH A BOW: *This caramel ganache was very smooth and buttery.*

$\mathscr{Z}$ELLER $\mathscr{C}$HOCOLATIER

PLACE LONGEMALLE 1, 1204 GENEVA, SWITZERLAND
TEL: (41-22) 311 5026

The fairies have long since vanished, but Willy Zeller has discovered their secret and continues makes Paves Glaces, the little chocolate slabs resembling the old Geneva paving stones, inspired by a fairy tale. His business was established in Geneva in 1959 at 13 Place Longemalle, and recently he moved into a bigger shop on the corner of Place Longemalle and the very fashionable Rue du Rhône. Here he still models marzipan figurines for the windows, which are decorated by his wife. For the last 20 years, they have been ably assisted by Madame

Monique Gimmi and her sister, Madame Brigitte Zentilin. Willy Zeller, the maître chocolatier, did his apprenticeship in Basle between 1936 and 1939, and has worked with many of the finest Swiss chocolatiers. Over the last 32 years, he has also been responsible for training many young chocolatiers.

The legend that was the inspiration for Zeller's famous Paves Glaces tells of a little girl enjoying the lakeside and watching men hauling quarried paving stones, shaped into cubes by masons, from the sailing boats that had carried them from the other side of the lake. The shiny stones were used in Geneva to build the streets on which horses and carriages rode. One of the two fairies who appeared before the girl was dressed in a pink, vanilla-scented gown. She said, "I am the Sweet Fairy who will make your dreams come true. Every paving stone you take in your hands will turn into chocolate." The second fairy blew gently on the stones and said, "I am the Bise (the name of the wind that blows on the lake, and also the word in French for a kiss) who makes glazed chocolate. Every time you eat chocolate you will think of the sweetness of Geneva and the cool of the lake."

USEFUL INFORMATION:

STAR RATING: ★★
COUNTRY OF ORIGIN: *Switzerland*
AVAILABILITY: *The shop in Geneva. Worldwide mail order.*
BOX SIZES: *Numerous*
HOUSE SPECIALTIES: *Paves glacés; over 70 different types of chocolates; Moules du Lac (mussels from the lake), large chocolates filled with caramel cream; marzipan figures: people, animals, fruit, vegetables, flowers; commissions and seasonal specialties for Christmas, Easter, and St. Valentine's Day.*
COUVERTURES USED:
Top secret

TASTING NOTES:

A 1950s style box—gold with a champagne-colored suede-effect lid—housed a selection of dark and milk chocolates. Without a doubt, the best in the selection were the dark or milk chocolate paves: very thin flat hard pieces of nougatine with almonds, dipped in chocolate. I preferred the milk chocolate to the dark, its creamy taste was the perfect foil to the crunchy brittle inside. These were very good, especially for those who like hard, nutty centers.

There were also very good oranges slices with peel dipped in dark chocolate; and an outstanding pistachio marzipan in dark chocolate. There was lots of variation in the fillings and plenty of dark chocolate.

MEDIUM-SIZED BRANDS

ACKERMANS

9 GOLDHURST TERRACE, FINCHLEY ROAD,
LONDON NW6 3HX, UK
TEL: (44-171) 624 2742

O ften traveling incognito, Ackermans chocolates often appear under other names in many of the most famous department stores, hotels, and restaurants in London and the United Kingdom. Started 50 years ago by German-born Werner Ackerman and his wife, the first shop was opened in Goldhurst Terrace, where all the chocolates were made. The business later expanded to a shop in Kensington Church Street (no longer open). The Queen Mother soon started ordering chocolates from Ackermans and in 1969, they were awarded her Royal Warrant.

Year-round specialty, a chocolate crocodile.

House specialties:
truffles and Swiss recipe chocolates.

USEFUL INFORMATION:

STAR RATING: ★ ★

COUNTRY OF ORIGIN: *Britain*

AVAILABILITY: *Concessions at Rackhams in Birmingham; Liberty in Regent Street, London, Sainsbury, Waitrose, and other leading grocery stores. Worldwide mail order: call the shop or the Chocolate Club: (44-171) 267 5375.*

BOX SIZES: *4 ounces to 3 pounds.*

HOUSE SPECIALTIES: *Seasonal specialties are Easter eggs, chickens, rabbits, Valentine hearts, St. Nicholas, and snowmen; also crocodiles, hippos, and lions; and chocolate champagne bottles filled with champagne truffles.*

COUVERTURES USED: *Callebaut and Lesme.*

One of the young Swiss chocolatiers who Mr. and Mrs. Ackerman took under their wing was Werner Kratiger. It was he who took over the business when Mr. Ackerman died. At this time all the chocolates were still being made in the tiny basement of the Goldhurst Terrace shop, and it was Kratiger who had the vision to move into a small industrial unit and to expand the business. From this new base and with his team of Valerie Miller, Franz Hippel, and Anthony Charlton, things went from strength to strength. Sadly, Kratiger died after a long illness three years ago, but the business is in good hands, as he had appointed Miller, Hippel, and Charlton directors of the company. As chocolate sales increase, the company remains faithful to the spirits of its forefathers, and Ackermans continues to make some of the finest chocolates in Britain.

Maître chocolatier Frank Hippel, who was born in 1961 in Busheim, Germany, served his apprenticeship in Spaichingen before coming to England in 1981. He started working for the famous Gloriette Pâtisserie, before joining Ackermans in 1982, where he worked under maître chocolatier, Werner Kratiger.

Hand-dipped crystallized orange slices and boxed chocolate crocodile.

TASTING NOTES:

Their Swiss recipe truffles came in all the traditional flavors: champagne, malt whiskey, cognac, rum, vanilla, and orange among them. Their handmade round wafers in mocha, mint, orange, and plain dark chocolate were exquisitely thin.

The almond, pistachio, and walnut pastes were from Lubecker in Germany, who have a reputation for producing the world's finest marzipan, and these are made into Mozart Kugeln—a rum truffle, with pistachio marzipan, dipped in dark chocolate and almonds.

The crystallized orange and lemon slices and sticks were hand-dipped; the Morello cherries soaked in brandy for a year and then dipped by the stalk into dark chocolate—beware: they still have their pits!

Traditional English recipes included rose and violet fondant creams in dark chocolate, caramels, crystallized stem ginger, and bittermints.

ANGELINA

226 RUE DE RIVOLI, 75001 PARIS, FRANCE
TEL: (33-1) 42 60 82 00/75 34   FAX: (33-1) 43 44 82 35

*R*umpelmayer's family business was founded in Nice in 1870 by Austrian-born Antoine Rumpelmayer, who later expanded the empire to Paris in 1903. His son René eventually took over, and it was he who was responsible for creating the legend of Angelina (his wife's name). Opposite the Tuileries Gardens in Paris, which boasts an outdoor skating rink in the winter, this famous chocolate house has been a meeting point for Parisian society since 1903: after René's death, Angelina received King George V of England; and Marcel Proust and Madame Coco Chanel frequently took tea at this fashionable watering hole.

Even with large premises on the Rue de Rivoli, there is still often a line here for tables. Morning coffee and chocolate are served, followed by light lunches, and then teas with sumptuous chocolate

USEFUL INFORMATION:

STAR RATING: ★★

COUNTRY OF ORIGIN: *France*

AVAILABILITY: *From the shop in Paris*

BOX SIZES: *10 ounces, 1 pound, and 1¼ pounds.*

HOUSE SPECIALTIES: *Hot chocolate. Tins of caramels and bonbons.*

COUVERTURES USED:

Top secret

TASTING NOTES:

On tasting these, I was pleasantly surprised at how good the chocolates were. There was a good selection of pralines, marzipans, and ganache centers which draw from the French, Austrian, and Swiss traditions.

In the selection was a gold-foiled pine cone, a milk chocolate praline which was smooth and sweet; a piped hazel gianduja, with a whole nut inside; cross-molded dark chocolate with pale coffee ganache inside; and pistachio marzipan with a good texture.

The oblong palet with a flat top revealed a sandwich of very good almond marzipan and a rum truffle. Also filled with a smooth rum truffle was the chocolate with a three-pointed star.

A lozenge with a yellow dot was lemon ganache, which had a very smooth chocolate and bits of lemon zest. It made a refreshing combination.

Rocher, with rich chocolate and almond chips on the outside, had a slightly grainy praline within; and a second dark praline had a crumbly center, again with very well-balanced, good, rich chocolate.

Chocolate bonbons, chocolate squares, and drinking chocolate from Angelina.

and cream cakes. Most famous of all are the jugs of thick, rich chocolat a l'Africain, which come with bowls of cold whipped cream. This drink is also sold in packets, so that you can make it at home, though it would be hard to recreate the period atmosphere found inside Angelina.

CÔTE DE FRANCE

9 AV DU PRÉSIDENT SALVADOR-ALLENDE,
VITRY-SUR-SEINE, 94400 FRANCE
TEL: (33-1) 46 80 85 06

ôte de France was founded in 1936, and the grandson of the founder continues a tradition of devotion to quality. "Quality . . . by excellence" has been the philosophy of the company since the outset. It is one of very few Parisian manufacturers that still makes chocolates starting from the cocoa beans—beans selected to give the chocolates a long, delicate finish. No artificial preservatives, coloring, or sweeteners are used, and the products are never deep-frozen. Since 1992 Côte de France has received various prizes at international food and chocolate fairs.

The maître chocolatier is Philippe Wasterlain. Having studied engineering, he learned the art of chocolate making during his school vacations, and apprenticed while continuing his studies, later to join the family firm that he continues to run. He is reputed to be one of the few chocolatiers to be able to taste unroasted beans and know what sort of blend they will make.

Box of assorted chocolate bonbons.

USEFUL INFORMATION:

STAR RATING: ★★

COUNTRY OF ORIGIN: *France*

AVAILABILITY: *6 shops in Paris, 8 shops and outlets in Japan, the flagship in Tokyo's Ginza. Mail order.*

BOX SIZES: *From about 7 ounces to 1 pound.*

HOUSE SPECIALTIES: *Additive-free produce; noisettines Dinantais; also enrobed cookies and pâté de fruit.*

COUVERTURES USED:

Only its own couverture, made from beans whose blend is a company secret. The majority come from South America and Indonesia. The big West African cocoa producers such as Cameroon and Ivory Coast are never used.

TASTING NOTES:

The dark, glossy chocolates displayed good workmanship and contained fine ingredients, but looked rather mass-produced, and all had praline centers. Inside the rather dull packaging were: a ship-embossed molded chocolate of dark praline, very fresh, crunchy not smooth.

A dark vine leaf of very good chocolate had a center hint of reglisse; a fatter leaf of milk chocolate had a very good smooth praline which was a bit too buttery.

The trapezoid shape of dark chocolate was a crunchy praline with a lingering aftertaste.

Two very smooth pralines were the four-leaf clover of coffee butter and praline, and the dark flower-printed square.

Other pralines included orange zest and crunchy nuts.

$\mathscr{D}$UDLE

WEGGISGASSE 34, LUCERNE CH-6004, SWITZERLAND
TEL: (41-41) 512767 FAX: (41-41) 512764

This is a small family business, started by Karl Habereli-Eizholzer in 1872, who was succeeded by his son, the young Edourd Dudle, who had first come to work as an apprentice in 1914. Dudle then spread his wings and traveled the world, finally gravitating toward the U.S. In 1934 he returned to take over the business, passing it on to his son Max in 1964. Today Max Dudle's son Martin is in charge and, keeping it in the family, has ensured that standards are maintained. No artificial preservatives or flavorings are used.

The maître chocolatier in charge of the 20 employees is Manfred Busch, and everything is still made by hand. Alongside the 1930's style chocolate shop, there is a tea room, where customers can relax. Dudle is most famous for its huge milk chocolate medallions, available in its shops.

USEFUL INFORMATION:

STAR RATING: ★★

COUNTRY OF ORIGIN: *Switzerland*

AVAILABILITY: *From the shop in Lucerne. Mail order.*

BOX SIZES: *Numerous*

HOUSE SPECIALTIES: *Dublones: a smooth filbert mousse set in creamy milk chocolate; Luzerne fish; milk chocolate filled with filbert praline; huge gold coins filled with a creamy, honey filling; assorted truffles; and solid chocolate bars with whole nuts.*

COUVERTURES USED: *Felchlin*

FASSBENDER

AM MARKT 12, 5200 SIEGBOURG, GERMANY
TEL: (49-2241) 66544   FAX: (49-2241) 66322

In 1910 Herr Fassbender started the first konditorei in Siegbourg, serving coffee, cakes, and chocolates. The business has remained in the family, and in 1989 Herr Fassbender's grandson, maître pâtissier Hans-Werner Fassbender was awarded membership of the famous International Association of Relais Desserts. He is one of only four pastry chefs in Germany today to be so honored. Fassbender also won the equivalent of the Nobel prize of the German bakery industry for his entrepreneurial skills in his very specialized trade. Fassbender spends 70 hours a week working—60 percent of his time in the kitchen, 30 percent in research development, and 10 percent in administration. In 1982 he opened a second shop in Köln, which inspired some of his Dom (Cathedral)-shaped chocolates and other confectioneries.

USEFUL INFORMATION:

STAR RATING: ★ ★

COUNTRY OF ORIGIN: *Germany*

AVAILABILITY: *From branches in Siegbourg, Bonn, and Köln. Worldwide mail-order catalog.*

BOX SIZES: *Numerous*

HOUSE SPECIALTIES: *Truffles, marzipans, tiny pyramid chocolate-covered cakes, Montélimar nougat, stöllen, and lebkuken.*

COUVERTURES USED: *Valrhona and Callebaut*

FAUCHON

26-28-30 PLACE DE LA MADELEINE, 75008 PARIS, FRANCE
TEL: (33-1) 47 42 60 11

orn in the Calvados region of Normandy in 1856, Auguste Fauchon left school at an early age to seek his fortune in Paris. There he set up a stand selling fruit and vegetables in the Madeleine. Fauchon prospered and was to remain in the area for the rest of his life. When he was 30 years old, he bought his first small shop in the Place de la Madeleine, Paris, which proved such an instant success that shortly afterward another two shops were acquired: nos. 24 & 26. The range and quality of the merchandise were without equal, and by 1925 there was a delicatessen, a pâtisserie, wine cellars, and a restaurant. To add to his talent for sourcing unusual and exclusive products, Fauchon also expanded his selection of merchandise by producing bottled fruits, jams, croissants, and French toast in his atelier, which he sold in his own shops and other carefully chosen outlets.

August Fauchon died in 1938, and the following 10 years of war and austerity were to undermine the business to the point of near bankruptcy. Fortunately it was rescued and taken over by Joseph Pilosoff, who remained faithful to the innovative ideology of Monsieur Fauchon. Exotic fruits and vegetables were flown in, producing surprises such as strawberries for sale at Christmas 1953, and the first avocados in France, which had to be given away because no one knew what they were.

Today the empire is led by Pilosoff's grand-daughter, Martine Premat, who has been chair and managing director since 1986. Now Fauchon goes from strength to strength. The legendary Pierre Hermé is the maître chocolatier. A fourth-generation boulanger and pâtissier, he left school at the age of 14 to become an apprentice at LeNôtre. At the age of 19, his talent was such that he was given overall responsibility for running the retail shop's production; then, during his Military Service, Hermé lost no time in disrupting the gray protocol he encountered in the Ministry of Defense kitchens. After setting up pastry kitchens for various shops and hotels in Paris, Luxembourg, and Brussels, he joined Fauchon in 1986. Hermé was given carte blanche to reorganize the whole pâtisserie section, and currently he heads a team of 35 patissiers and chocolatiers.

Pierre Hermé is famed for his original recipes and his adaptations of great classics. He says that he has witnessed the changes chocolate

Exquisite packaging by Fauchon.

has been undergoing, where the focus of attention has been on extremely dark and bitter chocolate with a minimum of 70 percent cocoa solids, and that some producers have gone overboard, using the percentage alone as an indicator of quality and making chocolate with 100 percent cocoa solids regardless of the quality of the cocoa beans. Hermé has always tried to put a brake on this "quest for the bitter," giving precedence to tempered bitterness, between 60 and 64 percent cocoa solids, which is the optimum percentage to maintain a balance between the different elements in chocolate, while allowing the full aroma of the cocoa beans to reveal themselves. However, Hermé is adamant that "with all the furore over black chocolate, we should not ignore milk chocolate." Traditionally of poor quality and the preserve of childhood memories, milk chocolate, with the help of one of the finest chocolate houses in the world—Valrhona—has undergone a renaissance. The best of these milk chocolates is Jivara Lactée. Hermé thinks it would seem churlish to ignore such a finely honed product, and he hopes therefore to be able to help numerous milk-chocolate lovers to come out of the closet without shame! Inspired by these thoughts, Hermé has created a cake with very little sugar, which allows the vanilla and caramel notes of the chocolate to shine through.

USEFUL INFORMATION:

STAR RATING: ★★★

COUNTRY OF ORIGIN: *France*

AVAILABILITY: *Specialty stores worldwide. Mail order.*

BOX SIZES: *Numerous*

HOUSE SPECIALTIES: *Chocolate marron glacés, cocoa truffles.*

COUVERTURES USED:

Valrhona: Caraïbe, Manjari, Guanaja, and Jivara Lactée.

TASTING NOTES:

The mainly flat square palet, *with cocoa butter transfers spelling out the letters "FAUCHON" on them, had a very fine layer of chocolate on each.*

F: *Was a dark crunchy praline in bitter chocolate and was well balanced.*

A: *Was of milk chocolate covering a smooth vanilla-laden praline—extremely good.*

U: *The dark chocolate, when cut open, revealed layers of smooth praline, and sandwiched in between was a sweet raspberry purée complete with seeds.*

C: *This most delicate cinnamon praline was delicious.*

H: *A ganache with caramel that was smooth, sweet, and buttery.*

O: *Was a milk chocolate crunchy praline.*

N: *Was a really excellent, smooth, coffee praline.*

FORTNUM & MASON

181 PICCADILLY, LONDON W1A 1ER
TEL: (44-171) 734 8040   FAX: (44-171) 437 3278

The history of Fortnum & Mason reaches back to 1707 when William Fortnum, footman in the Royal Household of Britain's Queen Anne, persuaded Hugh Mason to join him as a partner in setting up a grocery shop. Connected from the outset with service to the royal family, Fortnum & Mason has served twelve successive monarchs and has been involved in many events of historical significance, from supplying troops in the Napoleonic Wars to providing provisions for the first successful ascent of Mount Everest in 1953 and, more recently, during the Falkland and Bosnian conflicts.

Initially established to serve those fashionable townhouses built around St. James's Palace, Fortnum & Mason has specialized in providing the finest products and service, especially seeking out both the new and the exotic. Chocolate would have been one such item. From the mid-19th century, it first became a delicacy to be eaten, as well as a popular drink. Early records are incomplete, but by the late 1920s, when Mr. William Pain, the chocolatier first trained there, the chocolate department was fully established with the highest reputation. A Fortnum catalog from 1927 lists a choice of 50 chocolates, the majority of which are still available today and made with the same care and expertise.

From the outset, William Pain's flair was for confectionery, and at that stage, Fortnum & Mason was actually producing its own chocolate from the bean on an artisan scale. Importing fine cocoa beans from Trinidad, Java, and Maracaibo in Venezuela, expert Ted Nelson was responsible for roasting, conching, and refining the chocolate. William Pain found himself making ice creams for banquets and also the superb fruit in liqueur known as "orchards in the wine cellar," chocolate fondants, hand-dipped nuts, caramel, nougats, and marzipans

that were already part of the tradition of Fortnum & Mason chocolate and known today as its Superb Selection. It is a variety reflecting the marriage between the chocolatier and confectioner that is now regarded as typically British and is increasingly difficult to obtain as traditional craftsmanship bows out to mechanization and continental fashion. Sadly, of the "orchards in the wine cellar," only the brandied cherries survived World War II, and they are still made in the same fashion.

The war also saw Fortnum's creation of Service Chocolate in its distinctive pink wrapper. It was ordered by the Ministry of Food for officer's survival kits, and sent to Cyprus, thereby continuing the tradition of supplying servicemen abroad. It was this bitter chocolate that became the coating for another famous Fortnum & Mason line, the slimline peppermint with its distinctive soft green fondant.

By the start of World War II, the Fortnum &

Clockwise: *Icy Mints, Champagne Truffles, and Fortnum & Mason's Superb Selection.*

USEFUL INFORMATION:

STAR RATING: ★★
COUNTRY OF ORIGIN: *Britain*
AVAILABILITY: *From the shop in Piccadilly, London. Mail and telephone orders: (44-171) 465 8666.*
BOX SIZES: *8 ounces, 1 pound, up to 2¼ pounds.*
HOUSE SPECIALTIES: *Those described in Tasting Notes; Slimline Mints; After Dinner Selection; Royal Liqueurs; Rose and Violet creams; Elegant Thins available in cinnamon, ginger, coffee, orange, Earl Grey, and plain.*
COUVERTURES USED:
Top secret

William Pain and his wife retired and purchased a small chocolate factory, Audrey's, where traditions first learned in Piccadilly are still superbly practiced today. Chris Wolf remained at Fortnum & Mason until the 1980s when manufacture in Piccadilly finally ceased. In 1983, contact with Audrey's was made, and an old partnership renewed with much delight and pride on both sides.

Mason chocolate factory had been moved from Piccadilly to Brewer Street and was in the hands of Mr. Floris, a talented Hungarian refugee, who had by 1948, with William Pain as the general manager, formed a separate company, wholly supplying the shop. However, in 1948, the new Canadian owner of Fortnum & Mason decided to bring the chocolate production back to the fifth floor of the store and employed William Pain's No. 2, Chris Wolf. As a result, Floris Chocolatier was born and successfully found a market for its superb chocolates. The two factories and shops coexisted with the occasional change of temperamental chocolate dippers until 1961. When Mr Floris died,

TASTING NOTES:

LEMON SLICE: *A tangy crystallized slice of lemon with its peel, half-dipped in bitter chocolate makes a refreshing change to orange.*

VIOLET CREAM: *A single-dipped fondant cream topped with a whole crystallized violet has a powerful aroma of Parma violets which explodes in the mouth. Love it or hate it, it's impossible to be indifferent!*

HAZELNUT BATON: *A smooth rich dark chocolate covers delightfully crunchy toasted filberts.*

CHAMPAGNE TRUFFLE: *This was an extremely alcoholic milk chocolate ganache in the Swiss tradition.*

GRIOTTE: *A purple-foil-wrapped cherry in brandy, double-dipped by hand in rich dark chocolate, had a delightfully lopsided shape.*

ICY MINT: *A pale green fondant, with a strong mint flavor and dipped in extremely bitter chocolate, was a great example of the classic English chocolate mint.*

FRAN'S CHOCOLATES

2805 EAST MADISON, SEATTLE,
WASHINGTON 98122-4020
TEL: (206) 322-0233   FAX: (206) 322-0452

stablished in 1981, Fran's has quickly become known as a serious European-style chocolate maker, whose business was born from a passion for chocolate. Fran Bigelowe had a conventional start to her professional life, graduating and working as an accountant, who became very interested in cooking and pastry making only after her two children were born. She studied with the legendary octogenarian Josephine Araldo in San Francisco, who had graduated from the Cordon Bleu School in Paris in 1921, and had cooked for Clemenceau and Isadora Duncan. After her training with Araldo, Fran Bigelowe enrolled in the newly opened California Culinary Academy in 1976. All the time her children were growing up, she was passionately keen to start her own business. When the day arrived and the family moved back to Seattle in 1980, Fran invested her life savings and opened her shop in the Madison Park neighborhood. She says, "It's

evolved from one part of the spectrum all the way to another. In the beginning we were mainly doing desserts for restaurants. Today, it's evolved more and more into a chocolate line of candies and truffles that we've become known for, and we're proud that people are coming back for more." Fran is still very much involved with the chocolate making and more often than not can be found with chocolate-covered hands as she picks up an uncoated chocolate truffle, submerges the morsel in chocolate for a moment, lets the excess ooze through her spread fingers back into the tub, and then puts one perfect piece of candy on a tray.

USEFUL INFORMATION:

STAR RATING: ★★
COUNTRY OF ORIGIN: *U.S.*
AVAILABILITY: *From retail stores Williams-Sonoma, and Olsens in the U.S. Mail order.*
BOX SIZES: *2, 14, 28, 36, and 42 chocolates, and gift packages.*
HOUSE SPECIALTIES: *Dark chocolate truffles; Gold bars; hand-dipped fruit and nuts; a range of chocolate and caramel sauces, tortes, brownies and cheesecakes. Seasonal specialties of ginger, figs, and chocolate coins.*
COUVERTURES USED:
Callebaut

TASTING NOTES:

This line of dark chocolate truffles was extremely well finished, of glossy smooth chocolate with different finishes hand-drizzled onto them to distinguish the centers, although the differences between some of them were so subtle it was hard to distinguish them. Lightly whipped, very smooth, gentle, and creamy centers, were covered with well-balanced chocolate which, as one would expect from the Belgian tradition, was rich and dark without having any very strong characteristics or notes to finish on. I would be very interested to taste the same truffles made with French couverture.

HOTEL IMPERIAL

HOTEL IMPERIAL, KÄRTNER RING 16,
A-1051 VIENNA, AUSTRIA
TEL: (43-1) 50 110 313 OR 363   FAX: (43-1) 50 110 355

The Imperial Hotel is probably the grandest hotel in Vienna, originally built as a palace for the Duke of Württemberg and his wife, Maria Theresia. It was chosen as the venue for the World Exhibition in 1873, after which the hotel's status was raised to "Imperial and Royal" by the Emperor, Franz Joseph I. The Imperial torte was created for the inauguration of this event, and His Majesty is said to have declared, "It was indeed very good and brought us much pleasure." If you love almond paste and milk chocolate, this is the cake for you. Made without flour, it will last for two months in the refrigerator.

USEFUL INFORMATION:

STAR RATING: ★ ★

COUNTRY OF ORIGIN: *Austria*

AVAILABILITY: *From Hotel Imperial, Hotel Bristol, and Palais Ferstel in Vienna; Hotel Goldner Hirsch, Salzburg; Julius Meinl am Graben Deli, Vienna; Fukunaga's Lipton Tea Shop in Ginza, Tokyo.*

BOX SIZES: *2, 4, 9, and 16 portions in various boxes and wooden crates.*

House Specialties: *Imperial Torte*

COUVERTURES USED:

Top secret

La Maison du Chocolat

225 RUE FAUBOURG ST HONORÉ, PARIS 75008, FRANCE
TEL: (33-1) 42 27 39 44   FAX: (33-1) 47 64 03 75

Robert Linxe is one of the undisputed masters of the art of chocolate making in the world. When he moved to rue Faubourg St. Honoré, Linxe collaborated with fellow Basque artist and designer Arnaud Saez to create the distinctive masculine packaging and the corporate style of La Maison du Chocolat. At the age of 47, despite the risks of starting out on his own, Linxe knew that his individual creative urge was too strong to ignore. He also knew the direction in which he wanted to take French chocolate. Over the past two decades, Linxe has created an image of the finest French chocolate which will surely not be seen as a passing fad, for it is based on an appreciation of the complexities and subtleties of the cocoa bean that a discerning palate can understand. It is in this connection that we should look to his collaboration with Valrhona and their

Maître Chocolatier extraordinaire *Robert Linxe.*

commercial studies to become an apprentice pâtissier chocolatier, a rigorous training which was to stand him in good stead. For 3 years he worked from 8A.M. to 10P.M. However it was an initiation into the mysteries of a trade full of secrets and technical knowhow. By now truly fired with a passion, Robert Linxe decided that he had to be taught by the greater master Jules Perliat in Basle, Switzerland.

Having completed his studies, Linxe moved to Paris aged 25 and worked as a chocolatier in Neuilly. A year later, with the help of his parents-in-law, he took over an ailing chocolaterie, traiteur, and pâtisserie business La Marquise de Prèsle. After 5 years, things were on a solid footing, and a loyal clientele had been established. It was also a time of burgeoning competition which was emerging after years of austerity, but Linxe held his own and started to

production of a line of Grand Cru couvertures, which are in my opinion the benchmark by which all other fine dark chocolates should be measured. Fine chocolate will never reach quite the same degree of complexity as fine wine, but Robert Linxe has been instrumental in bringing it to a position where it can be enjoyed by chocoholics and wine buffs alike.

Production has since moved from the wine cellars of the original shop to a purpose-built unit at Colombes on the outskirts of Paris with 18 employees including 10 full time chocolatiers.

Growing up in the Basque region of France, which has a long tradition of chocolate making, must have had an influence, for in 1949 at the age of 18, Linxe decided to change from

USEFUL INFORMATION:

STAR RATING: ★ ★ ★
COUNTRY OF ORIGIN: *France*
AVAILABILITY: *Paris, New York, and Neiman-Marcus in Houston and Dallas.*
BOX SIZES: *14 ounces, 1¼ pounds, 1¼ pounds, and 2¼ pounds.*
HOUSE SPECIALTIES: *Those described in Tasting Notes.*
COUVERTURES USED: *Valrhona*

*Robert Linxe's classic chocolate box
inspired by Hérmes.*

receive recognition from a wider and wider client base. He also had encouraging reviews in the press, and in 1970 Linxe was invited to Japan on a professional trip where he met Gaston LeNôtre, probably his strongest competition in Paris. LeNôtre quickly proposed a partnership with Linxe, and they began to work together.

In his heart of hearts, Linxe felt that by joining LeNôtre he had let his faithful customers down, so in 1977, when he heard of a wine merchant's for sale in the rue Faubourg St. Honoré, opposite the famous concert hall Les Salles Pleyelle, he branched out on his own. It was an old shop with large wine cellars, which proved very suitable for chocolate production, and above all the location was to be the inspiration of the many of his chocolate creations that have their musical counterparts: Bohème, Rigoletto, Faust, Traviata, Otello, Romeo, and Sylvia. The location also ensured a clientele of artists.

TASTING NOTES:

RIGOLETTO: *A thin square with a stripe along the diagonal, the milk chocolate couverture had inside it a caramelized butter. The flavor of the caramel is designed to set off the creaminess of the couverture.*

MONT-BLANC: *The conical milk chocolate pyramid with a white nipple on top had a ganache made with a whipped butter and flavored with kirsch. This is an adaptation of a Swiss recipe learned in 1952.*

LISELOTTE: *This is a praline with a milk chocolate couverture, lozenge shaped with lines along the length. The praline is almost a gianduja, made with ¼ filberts to ¼ almonds.*

GUAYAQUIL: *A large flat square, with a slightly wavy surface had a dark couverture with semibitter ganache made with Ecuadorian beans. It had some vanilla notes and was very light.*

QUITO: *A bright shining palet of a very fine dark chocolate coating had a ganache with a very powerful aroma and very long finish due to the mix of Venezuelan, Ecuadorian, Trinidadian, and Madagascan beans.*

ANDALOUSIE: *Inside a rectangle with dark couverture, the ganache was made from three types of* criollo *beans—Venezuelan, Caribbean, and Ecuadorian. This was delicately flavored with lemon, a match less easy to make than that of chocolate and orange.*

ROMÉO: *This was a dark chocolate couverture rectangle with stripes across the width, and the ganache was a butter mocha, the coffee flavor coming from freshly filtered coffee.*

$\mathscr{M}$OONSTRUCK $\mathscr{C}$HOCOLATIER

6663 SW BVTN-HILLSDALE HIGHWAY,
STE 194, PORTLAND, OREGON 97225
TEL: (503) 283-8843   FAX: (503) 283-8913

his very slick marketing company has an impressive panel of experts: Dean Stearman, former marketing director of Godiva USA (also former vice president of Barton Chocolates); Dr. Schouten, professor of Marketing at the University of Portland, who is also a behavioral market-research analyst for companies including Harley-Davidson "the ultimate mean motorbike;" and William Simmons, the founder of the company, who has extensive experience in the food industry. Simmons had concluded in earlier research that "there is a direct link between the changes that started . . . in the coffee industry (in the U.S.) of the 80s, relative to fine beans, and an opportunity of similar proportions awakening in the chocolate industry in the 90s." These gentlemen have plans to take the U.S. chocolate market by storm. The packaging is fun and beautifully produced. The chocolates are made with great care and ingenuity, and the "book" box, certain to become a collector's item, states the company's aims and objectives in fairy-tale

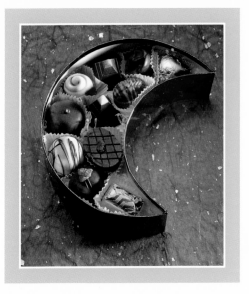

Moonstruck's hallmark moon-shaped box.

language in the opening pages: "Much like Merlin, who aged backward in King Arthur's Camelot, and thus knew what the future held, Moonstruck Chocolatier started out with the common chocolate of today. They then researched backward, looking for the non-sweet purity of the chocolate of the past.

"One sad fact stood out. In 94 percent of today's chocolate, the cocoa bean of old has been replaced by a bean that has little character.

"The best cocoa beans, when properly prepared, yield chocolate with qualities that verge on the mystical. Disregarding cost, Moonstruck Chocolatier begins with its unique blend of chocolate, then enhances it with the freshest

USEFUL INFORMATION:

STAR RATING: ★★

COUNTRY OF ORIGIN: *United States*

AVAILABILITY: *112 outlets around the U.S. Mail order.*

BOX SIZES: *4, 6, 8, or 16 pieces and 1 pound box*

HOUSE SPECIALTIES: *Moon-shaped boxes, a selection of truffles and chocolates including wine, brandy, saké, fruit, and coffee.*

COUVERTURES USED:
It sources chocolate liquors and makes its own couverture, adding 38 to 40 percent coc butter and selecting fine and flavorful bean varicies.

the chocolate directory

flavors and the creativity that has come to characterize the Pacific Northwest. Award-winning wines, robust espressos, fresh creams, wholesome fruits, and distilled brandies have all brought worldwide acclaim to the region called home by Moonstruck Chocolatier.

"Moonstruck's elegant creations are meant to celebrate the purity of olde-worlde chocolate and the whimsical spirit of life."

The chocolates live up to the sales and marketing pitch and are produced with great care and attention, albeit on a semi-industrial scale. These chocolates may not really be the vehicle for launching fine flavor beans on the American market, but if they help raise questions in the mind of the chocolate lover about the origin of the cocoa beans, they have already won half the battle.

The maître chocolatier is Robert Hammond, who apprenticed under a master chocolatier in the southern U.S., after which he studied in France, and completed his European tour by working in Italy, the Netherlands, Britain, and the Middle East. Returning to the U.S., he worked in many of the top hotels and then became chef at the Vanderbilt Estate (the largest

U.S. private home). Hammond is now a leading expert in the field of chocolate and confectionery.

TASTING NOTES:

The samples I tasted were very well made, the fillings well balanced and sensual with a sense of fun. I must confess that although the chocolate itself was smooth and melting, without any unpleasant "notes," the fillings and the use of a fair amount of milk chocolate meant that it was hard to distinguish any rare flavor beans in the chocolate.

MILK CHOCOLATE HEART: *Filled with pecan gianduja and soft caramel—this was very good, delicate, and not too sweet.*

SOKOL BLOSSER WINE TRUFFLE: *The ganache was very good with lots of fruit—a successful and interesting combination.*

WILD HUCKLEBERRY TRUFFLE: *A jam-like filling and a white chocolate ganache resulted in a very sweet chocolate.*

GIANDUJA ALMOND PRALINE TOWER: *This had a very good, crisp butter toffee and roasted almonds.*

STACH TEA TRUFFLE: *This was a well-balanced ganache with caramel and Earl Grey.*

CLEAR CREEK APPLE BRANDY TRUFFLE: *This was a very subtle caramelly truffle.*

PURE GOLD TRUFFLE: *This bittersweet ganache, the filling darker than the covering, and with honey and Drambuie, looked very dramatic, especially with the gold leaf embellishment.*

ESPRESSO ITALIA TRUFFLE: *Tasting like a cup of capuccino, it had good flavor and silky texture.*

PRESTAT

14 PRINCES ARCADE, PICCADILLY, LONDON SW1Y 6DS, UK
TEL: (44-171) 629 4838

One of London's oldest established chocolate houses, first established in 1902 in Oxford Street, has suffered many takeovers and changes of location, but it re-emerged in Princes Arcade in the 1980s. Their truffle recipe is a family secret dating back to the time of Napoleon III, but unfortunately Prestat no longer makes its own chocolates.

USEFUL INFORMATION:

STAR RATING: ★

COUNTRY OF ORIGIN: *Britain*

AVAILABILITY: *Mail-order catalog*

BOX SIZES: *8 ounces, 12 ounces, 1 pound, 1½ pounds, and 2 pounds.*

HOUSE SPECIALTIES: *The Connoisseur selection of chocolates; and Brandy Cherries.*

COUVERTURES USED:

Top secret

COMMERCIAL BRANDS

ℬARATTI & ℳILANO

VIA NANNETTI 1, 40069 ZOLA PREDOSA (BOLOGNA), ITALY
TEL: (39-51) 617 2777   FAX: (39-51) 617 2769

A relative newcomer to gianduja production, this house was founded in 1858 by Ferdinando Baratti and Eduardo Milano. In 1875 the Lord Mayor officiated at a presentation of the Royal Family's coat of arms, which Baratti & Milano have used ever since on their logo. The shop drew huge crowds, and one attraction was the huge mirror, apparently the largest in Italy. The shop was also a focal point for many artists, politicians, scientists, and writers at this time, including a prominent doctor who helped to increase sales by recommending consumption of the shop's chocolates for their restorative qualities!

USEFUL INFORMATION:

STAR RATING: ★★

COUNTRY OF ORIGIN: *Italy*

AVAILABILITY: *In specialist Italian gourmet stores.*

BOX SIZES: *Numerous*

HOUSE SPECIALTIES: *Giandujotti, Cremeni, Milord, and Medagliato; and Easter eggs.*

COUVERTURES USED: *A high and fine quality, made with American and African cocoa beans.*

$\mathscr{B}$ENDICKS OF $\mathscr{M}$AYFAIR

46 CURZON STREET, LONDON W1Y 7RF, UK

TEL: (44-171) 629 4389

$\mathscr{F}$ounded in 1921 by a Colonel Benson and a Mr. Dickson, Bendick's was originally a confectioner and pastry maker. The chocolate, however, became so popular that the pastrymaking was dropped. The name was certainly created by adding the "BEN" from Colonel Benson's name to the "DICKS" from Mr. Dickson, though the recipe for the Bittermint was apparently invented by Benson's sister-in-law, and is without a doubt Bendick's most famous product, much imitated by other chocolate makers. A sublime, potent firm mint fondant made from pure essential peppermint oil, which bought by the ounce is more expensive than a fine malt whiskey, the mint is then dipped in unsweetened chocolate. It is the perfect end to a rich meal and has a soothing, almost medicinal quality, much beloved by the British population—royals and lesser mortals alike. In 1962 Bendicks was granted a Royal Warrant by Queen Elizabeth II. It is reputedly the favorite chocolate of the Princess of Wales, the Queen Mother, and the Duke of Kent, and can be found in all the guest bedrooms at Sandringham, the Queen's Norfolk home.

Now owned by the German-based confectionery manufacturer August Stork KG, the company continue to produce a wide range of chocolate-dipped fruit fondants, fudge, caramels, and nuts. Much hand-finishing still goes on, and there are some recipes which are so delicate that they have defeated all efforts to be automated; they can be found in the Superfine selection.

USEFUL INFORMATION:

STAR RATING: ★★

COUNTRY OF ORIGIN: *Britain*

AVAILABILITY: *From their own 4 stores in central London, as well as in all major department stores, such as Selfridges, Fortnum & Mason, John Lewis, Waitrose, Safeway, Tesco, J. Sainsbury's throughout the UK.*

BOX SIZES: *Numerous*

HOUSE SPECIALTIES: *Mint collection, Bittermints, Mint Crisps, Chocolate Peppermint Creams, White Chocolate Mints.*

COUVERTURES USED:

They make their own, using fine flavored West Indian beans for their Sporting and Military plain chocolate and Bittermints. The couverture used for dipping the centers is made from West African beans.

TASTING NOTES:

BITTERMINT: *This is a single enrobed unsweetened chocolate and refreshing mint fondant. The ultimate chocolate mint.*

CREME DE MENTHE: *This chocolate is altogether more tempered in its components: a bittersweet chocolate, filled with a soft green mint fondant.*

THE MINT CRISP: *This mint-flavored chocolate circle studded with granules of crunchy honeycomb is a delicate crunchy confection.*

THE MAYFAIR MINT: *This mint should not be tackled by the faint-hearted—do not try to break it as I did, or your hands will be covered in sticky mint fondant and chocolate shards. Put the whole thing into your mouth!*

THE VICTORIA MINT: *This is another sweet, firm peppermint fondant, covered with thick dark dessert chocolate.*

CAFFAREL

VIA GIANEVELLO 41, 10062 LUSERNA, S. GIOVANNI
(TO), ITALY
TEL: (39) 121 90 03 44   FAX: (39) 121 90 18 53

One of Europe's oldest established chocolate houses, it was Caffarel that inspired the Swiss youth François Louis Cailler to set up the first chocolate factory in Switzerland. Even in the early 1800s, there was much cross-border trade between Italy and Switzerland, and it was at a Swiss village fair that Cailler first smelled the fragrant mixture of chocolate and filberts being made by Caffarel. So enthralled was the young Cailler that he begged to be taken back to Italy to learn the trade of chocolate making. He trained at Caffarel for four years before returning to Switzerland as a maître chocolatier. (In 1819 Cailler designed and built a cocoa press complete with stone roller, and he opened the first Swiss chocolate factory at Corsier near Vevey.)

The Caffarel factory was opened outside Turin in the early 1800s, situated next to a river which harnessed the water power in order to drive the hydraulic wheel and cocoa mill. The exact dates are a bit hazy, but an early newspaper clipping from around this time confirms that "Caffarel Father & Son—have purchased from Bozelli of Genoa a machine to make chocolate." Having taken the path leading to industrialization, the company began growing into a truly modern concern, although it would never set aside the spirit of artisanship that was by now so deeply engrained.

Caffarel invented gianduiotti in 1852. It produced this new variety of chocolate by blending cocoa powder and sugar, with Piedmont's celebrated round and fragrant filberts. The name came from the word "givu" (in Piedmont dialect), which became "gianduiotto," a nickname destined to win the acclaim of gourmets and gluttons around the world.

The process that used to be performed completely by hand, forcing the chocolate through a pastry bag into molds, is now done by a

specially designed machine. The result is deceptive; the gianduiotti still look as if they have been made by hand.

TASTING NOTES:

Caffarel's products are of exemplary quality, the gianduiotti are smooth and nutty, and melt perfectly in the mouth, without a trace of greasiness, and the Croccante Gentile is one of the best croquants made from filberts that you are likely to find.

USEFUL INFORMATION:

STAR RATING: ★ ★
COUNTRY OF ORIGIN: *Italy*
AVAILABILITY: *Widely available in specialty shops, in 32 countries around the world.*
BOX SIZES: *Numerous*
HOUSE SPECIALTIES: *Gianduia 1865; Noblesse, filbert foiled squares; box of assorted pralines; but best of all are the beautiful blue and gold cans, filled with the gianduiotti, and the blue and white tin filled with individually paper-wrapped Croccante Gentile. Seasonal specialties: red-foiled chocolate roses, hearts, ladybugs, and bumblebees; gold bars and money; large and small Easter eggs.*
COUVERTURES USED:
Made in-house using directly imported cocoa beans, the rarest of them being the Esmeralda from Ecuador and Angoleta from Samoa.

Traditional cans filled with Gianduiotti.

CHARBONNEL ET WALKER

1 THE ROYAL ARCADE, 28 OLD BOND STREET,
LONDON W1X 4BT, UK
TEL: (44-171) 491 0939   FAX: (44-171) 495 6279

*I*t was Edward VII who encouraged Madame Charbonnel to leave her Paris chocolate house, Maison Boissier, to join Mrs. Walker in London in order to establish a fine confectionery house there. It opened in 1875, and because the shop has always held a Royal Warrant, it has been the victim of many acquisitions and mergers. In 1989 the company returned to private ownership and introduced an innovative selection of chocolate truffle sauces, molinillos, jugs, and drinking chocolate, which keep the same corporate image and packaging style of their established lines.

In some ways the packaging is an outstanding feature of these chocolates, but since their acquisition of the Belgian Maxwell & Kennedy chain, a number of unwelcome changes in the line of chocolates have been witnessed. Although their classic Rose and Violet creams remain some of the finest examples of their genre, anything in a molded shell will almost certainly be a "continental" style filling, an area which I feel is moving away from Charbonnel's fine English tradition. Charbonnel has, however, maintained its tradition of Boites Blanches: huge round boxes which contain messages spelled out on foil-wrapped chocolates. Their numbered chocolate system dates back to 1901, in which customers may pick their own personal selection, ensuring that no unwanted "surprise" centers creep in. They have not just one, but five, maître chocolatiers of equal standing.

Truffle-filled chocolate champagne bottle and enrobed espresso.

USEFUL INFORMATION:

STAR RATING: ★★
COUNTRY OF ORIGIN: *Britain*
AVAILABILITY: *From many delicatessens throughout Britain and mail-order catalog.*
BOX SIZES: *4 ounces, 8 ounces, 1 pound, 1½ pounds, 2 pounds, 3 pounds, 4 pounds, up to 10 pounds.*
HOUSE SPECIALTIES: *Enrobed coffee beans, Bittermints, Mint Crisps, Mocha Batons, Maple Brazils, Cremes Parisiennes, and Chocolate Stem Ginger are all enduring classics; chocolate champagne bottle filled with champagne truffles; novelties at Christmas and Easter.*
COUVERTURES USED:
Top secret

TASTING NOTES:
The classics included Rose Cream: an excellent, firm, highly perfumed fondant in good dark chocolate; and stem ginger in dark chocolate—a good, crunchy-textured, strong, and slightly hot ginger. A walnut-topped chocolate contained a walnut ganache of good texture. Two nutty chocolates were a chocolate Brazil nut with a crisp Brazil and good dark chocolate; and an almond marzipan with slight banana notes.

A baton, which looked like it might have been orange peel, was in fact a very hard and crunchy nougatine coated in dark chocolate.

The truffles included a whipped vanilla mousse; an artificial-tasting whipped orange; a grainy-textured, whipped, milky filling; and a very sweet bubblegum or possibly, Champagne-flavored whipped truffle in dark chocolate.

$\mathscr{C}$HOCOLATERIE
$\mathscr{B}$ERNARD $\mathscr{C}$ALLEBAUT

1313 - 1ST STREET SE, CALGARY, ALBERTA,
CANADA T2G 5L1
TEL: (403) 265-5777

$\mathscr{B}$ernard Callebaut is the fourth generation of the famous Belgian chocolate manufacturing family, born in Wieze in 1954. Following the death of Bernard Callebaut's father and uncle in the late 1970s, the company had a crisis of direction, and there were many conflicting ideas from the various interested members of the family about what to do with the business. Finally it was agreed to accept the offer made by the Swiss giants; the Suchard Toblerone group, and the proceeds were divided up between the Callebauts. For Bernard Callebaut, this was a wonderful opportunity to spread his wings and move away from the restrictive business atmosphere in Belgium. He was invited by a former customer of the chocolate factory, based in Antwerp, to come and learn the art of making cream and butter fillings, after which he spent a year traveling the world, with an eye to finding a suitable location for his new venture.

In 1983 Callebaut emigrated to Canada and set up shop in Calgary, against the advice of many locals who did not believe that such expensive, sophisticated, European chocolates would find a market. Bernard, however, had a good hunch that the colder the climate, the higher the chocolate consumption. He was proved right, for after a steady start to the business, turning over $200,000 in the first year, and doubling in the second year, the growth has been phenomenal, now topping $3,000,000, and this upward trend is set to continue as he opens more franchises and supplies stores across the U.S.

USEFUL INFORMATION:

STAR RATING: ★ ★

COUNTRY OF ORIGIN: *Canada*

AVAILABILITY: *20 dealers in Canada, 3 of their own outlets, more planned. Mail order throughout the U.S.*

BOX SIZES: *Numerous*

HOUSE SPECIALTIES: *47 different centers, with an additional 20 varieties in peak season. Molded Santa Claus and other seasonal shapes.*

COUVERTURES USED:

Callebaut couverture from Belgium.

TASTING NOTES:

The chocolates were molded shells, filled with classic Belgian buttercream centers. The Amaretto was a very soft, smooth buttercream, without any distinct flavor, but with a good smooth dark chocolate shell.

The Rum Cup had a dark shell, a double layer inside, and a rich smooth milk chocolate center, while the chestnut-shaped shell was filled with a sweet green fondant cream.

A dark chocolate case with a whipped praline, topped with a filbert, was certainly the most interesting. Others tasted similar, but the semi-liquid fondant creams were my least favorite as they were very sweet.

CAMILLE BLOCH

CH-2608 COURTELARY, SWITZERLAND
TEL: [41] 39 44 17 17   FAX: [41] 39 44 10 38

amille Bloch started making chocolates in his kitchen at home in Bern in 1929, using ready-made couverture. It was the same year as the Wall Street Crash and marked the start of the worldwide Depression. Four years later, Bloch set up production of chocolate from cocoa beans, in the face of much competition from the old "pioneers," by now well established. During World War II, there was a great shortage of raw materials, especially cocoa beans, so Camille Bloch put his mind to inventing a new product and, sourcing supplies of almonds and filberts from Turkey and Spain, he created Ragusa, a forerunner of their famous Torino bar, made from praline.

Camille Bloch's son Rolf later took over the business, although his father continued to be involved until his death at the age of 80. Now producing 14¾ tons of chocolate every day, this company ranks as the fourth-largest chocolate producer in Switzerland. In spite of its size, the

House specialties, Kirsch-li.

company is still run as ordained by Camille Bloch, and the workforce of 200 have a variety of benefits offered to them, from accommodation, health care, and a special company pension to a restaurant and in-house magazine.

Camille Bloch is not, however, aiming to become a multinational company. It wants to stay small enough to guarantee daily quality control and keep in close touch with its customers and the market—a refreshing attitude these days!

USEFUL INFORMATION:

STAR RATING: ★ ★
COUNTRY OF ORIGIN: *Switzerland*
AVAILABILITY: *Widely available in Europe, North America, and Southeast Asia.*
BOX SIZES: *4 ounces, 8 ounces, and 1 pound.*
HOUSE SPECIALTIES: *Those described in Tasting Notes; seasonal specialties of Kirsch-li, Truffle Buchette, and Ragusa Jubilee.*
COUVERTURES USED:
They make their own.

TASTING NOTES:

The chocolates I tasted were very fresh, glossy, and much more delicious than I was expecting. They gave a strong, possibly artificial, vanilla aroma, with a cool melting sensation in the mouth, reminiscent of the Pyrenéen chocolates of bygone days.

There was a good crunchy praline with a very fresh toasted filbert on top; some very sweet little Neapolitans, in the different flavors of Café, Torino, Zarbitter, and Cric Crac; and liqueurs without the sugar crust.

······ ● ······

CONFISERIE HEINEMANN

KREFELDER STRASSE 645, 41066 MÖNCHEN-GLADBACH,
GERMANY   TEL: (49) 2161 6930

The town of Mönchen-Gladbach, probably most famous for its soccer team, saw the opening of a konditorei, a coffee house serving pastries and confectionery, in 1932. Opened by Hermann Heinemann, the business grew slowly at first; in fact, it came to a complete standstill during World War II, but in 1953 Heinemann took the step of making his own chocolates. So successful were they that by 1966 he had 6 shops in 4 different cities, and it became apparent that a large, modern production unit was needed to supply the growing needs of these shops.

As soon as they were old enough, Heinemann's two sons joined the business, but sadly Bernd Heinemann met an untimely death in 1992. These days Heinz Richard Heinemann is not only the dynamic chairman of the company, boasting 11 shops, he is also maître chocolatier and member of

Maître chocolatier Heinz Richard Heinemann.

USEFUL INFORMATION:

STAR RATING: ★ ★

COUNTRY OF ORIGIN: *Germany*

AVAILABILITY: *11 shops around Germany. Worldwide mail order.*

BOX SIZES: *A huge array!*

HOUSE SPECIALTIES: *Over 60 varieties of chocolate made freshly every day, including orange, cocoa, almond, walnut, kirsch, nougat, and croquant. Seasonal specialties: Santa Claus in many different outfits, Valentine's hearts, Easter eggs, flower bouquets, clowns, animals, and other fun characters filled with chocolates.*

COUVERTURES USED: *They make their own.*

the International Association of Relais Desserts. Heinz Richard learned the art of chocolate making over a 10-year period.

TASTING NOTES:

An exceptional Champagne truffle was dusted with powdered sugar, and inside the milk chocolate shell it was made up of two halves. It had a light melting buttercream full of alcohol, and a milk chocolate ganache.

A square premolded cup filled with a buttery liquid caramel, and topped with an almond croquant, looked very industrial but had an excellent flavor, especially if you love caramel and milk chocolate.

The milk chocolate truffle with white stripes tasted of a very strong orange alcohol, and lacked subtlety, as did the Cognac truffles.

CUBA

12100 CUNEO, PIAZA EUROPA 14, ITALY
TEL: (39-171) 26 42 45   FAX: (39-171) 26 40 08

his family-run company is now into the third generation. Started by Pietro Cussino, who was born in 1917, and one of 9 children, the name Cuba presumably refers to the chocolate cigars which the company make. The company has been awarded a warrant of purity and quality by the Italian Celiac Association (celiacs require gluten-free products).

USEFUL INFORMATION:

STAR RATING: ★

COUNTRY OF ORIGIN: *Italy*

AVAILABILITY: *Greece, Australia, South America, Germany, France, Britain.*

BOX SIZES: *Numerous*

HOUSE SPECIALTIES: *Gianduiotti; Tartufo (truffle); Pistacchio—a chocolate with almond and pistachio; Crocantino; leaves and flowers made in chocolate; chocolate orange peel.*

COUVERTURES USED:

Made in-house, using beans from Guayaquil (Ecuador), Venezuela, and Ghana.

$\mathscr{D}$REIMEISTER

WESTSTRASSE 47·49 – D-59457 WERL, WESTÖNNEN,
GERMANY
TEL: (49-2922) 8 20 45   FAX: (49-2922) 8 52 52

$\mathscr{S}$tarted in 1953 by the father of the present maître chocolatier, Hans Wilhelm Scröder, Dreimeister was known as Café Scröder. Its original location was in the shadow of the Basilica in the pilgrim town of Werl. The name Dreimeister was adopted in 1973, and the large production unit was opened in 1988 in a converted dairy. In spite of a large turnover, the company prides itself on using only quality and fresh raw materials—nothing is more than 7 days old when it reaches the customer.

USEFUL INFORMATION:

STAR RATING: ★ ★

COUNTRY OF ORIGIN: *Germany*

AVAILABILITY: *Hotels, restaurants, specialty food shops, airlines, and mail order.*

BOX SIZES: *Numerous*

HOUSE SPECIALTIES: *Truffles and seasonal Christmas trees and stars.*

COUVERTURES USED: *Callebaut and Cacao Barry.*

GODIVA

RUE DE L'ARMISTICE 5, B-1080 BRUSSELS, BELGIUM
TEL: (LONDON) (44-171) 495 2845
FAX: (44-171) 409 0963

To many people around the world, Godiva represents the finest chocolate money can buy, and this chocolate is especially popular in the U.S. This huge chocolate empire was founded in 1929 by the Draps family. The business was bought outright in 1966 by Campbell's Soup and is now a huge industrial concern, with 1,400 branches worldwide. The chocolates are made by two factories: one in Belgium, which supplies the European markets; the other in Pennsylvania, which makes chocolates especially designed for the American market. The recipes differ according to the market.

A selection of pralines from Godiva.

STAR RATING: ★

COUNTRY OF ORIGIN: *Belgium and U.S.*

AVAILABILITY: *Worldwide mail order, fine stores, and Godiva stores.*

BOX SIZES: *8 ounces to 2 pounds, also luxury boxes up to 4 pounds.*

HOUSE SPECIALTIES: *"All are special—particularly the Belgian Pralines": Dame Blanche, Autant, Truffle Amere, Cerisette, Coeur de Bruxelles, Milk and Dark, Truffle Fine Champagne, Cascade, Carre Godiva, and Raisin Fine Champagne. Seasonal specialties are chocolate bears, buchettes, small and large logs, and special shapes of chestnut and walnut with orange praline.*

COUVERTURES USED:

Milk, white, and dark varieties made from Godiva's own patent recipe.

TASTING NOTES:

The chocolates I tasted were from Belgium: they were large, well made, and well presented in elegant, simple packaging. Good dark milk and white chocolate surrounded very sweet centers. Vegetable fat, real and artificial vanilla were listed in the ingredients.

I tasted a dark chocolate heart, with a very thick shell which had praline inside; and a cocoa-dusted truffle, that may have been double-dipped, with a milk with vanilla rum, that was too sweet for me.

Another dusted truffle, the first skin dark, then a milk layer, had inside it a smooth milky truffle; and the milk chocolate circle with a piped dark chocolate leaf on top had a soft caramel center with a hint of coffee.

A white frog cluster with a nutty dusting and a whipped up, pale, grainy praline filling had crunchy sugar which, again, I found too sweet.

HOTEL SACHER

HOTEL SACHER VIENNA A-1010 WIEN,
PHILHARMONIKERSTRAβE 4, AUSTRIA
TEL: (43-1) 51456   FAX: (43-1) 51457

The most famous of all chocolate cakes, the Sachertorte, was invented in 1832 by a 16-year-old kitchen boy, Franz Sacher, who was undergoing his apprenticeship at the time. The young Sacher went on to work at Esterhàzy Palace, taking his secret recipe with him. He and the cake were much in demand, and by the age of 30, having made a small fortune, Sacher returned to his native Vienna and opened a delicatessen behind St. Stephen's Cathedral.

It was Sacher's son who opened the celebrated Hotel Sacher, which has survived in its present location for well over 100 years, although it has undergone numerous facelifts.

USEFUL INFORMATION:

STAR RATING: ★ ★

COUNTRY OF ORIGIN: *Austria*

AVAILABILITY: *From the Hotel Sacher. Worldwide mail order.*

BOX SIZES: *Not applicable*

HOUSE SPECIALTIES: *Sachertorte*

COUVERTURES USED:

Top secret

$\mathscr{J}$OSEPH $\mathscr{S}$CHMIDT
$\mathscr{C}$ONFECTIONS

3489 16TH ST, SAN FRANCISCO CALIFORNIA 94114
TEL: (415) 861-8682   FAX: (415) 861-3923

he first shop opened by Joseph Schmidt and Audrey Ryan in 1983 expanded so rapidly that production had to move to larger premises, where over 150 personnel—mainly women—are employed. The rationale behind this policy is not as sexist as it sounds, it is merely biological: women naturally have cooler hands than men, temperature fluctuations of just one or two degrees can be critical in chocolate making, and all the decorative work on these truffles is done by hand. Joseph Schmidt chocolates look stunning and are probably the most daring, without being over-the-top, that I have ever seen. Audrey Ryan designs and develops the packaging, and also executes the more architectural commissions.

Signature truffle selection from Joseph Schmidt.

Maître chocolatier Joseph Schmidt was born in 1939 of Austrian parents and grew up in Palestine. Schmidt does not, however, think of himself as Israeli, drawing more inspiration from his Austrian roots, and that country's tradition of great cakes and chocolates. Trained as a baker, with no formal chocolate apprenticeship, Schmidt eschews the idea of being the pupil of a maître chocolatier: "I don't follow a master's tradition—in Europe everyone learns from a master and follows it like a bible, I like to break tradition. It's just as much fun as keeping it. [Chocolate] is the most fun material in the food business. It gets soft quickly, you play with it, and in a few minutes it's hard as a rock. I would think a lot of creative people would be drawn to chocolate for that reason, but I've been disappointed. The chocolate industry is very, very conservative. Confectioners in

USEFUL INFORMATION:

STAR RATING: ★ ★ ★

COUNTRY OF ORIGIN: *United States*

AVAILABILITY: *From the store in San Francisco, and at Neiman Marcus, Macy's, Nordstrom, Saks Fifth Avenue, Williams-Sonoma throughout the U.S. Quarterly mail order catalog for the home market. Harrods in London.*

BOX SIZES: *Numerous*

HOUSE SPECIALTIES: *Valentine's Day, Easter, Mother's Day, Summer, Father's Day, Autumn, Thanksgiving, and Christmas.. Special commissions include: a white dove for Nelson Mandela; a giant panda for Prince Philip; a wedding anniversary present for President Reagan commissioned by Nancy Reagan; the Eiffel Tower for the French Ambassador; and a gift for Mikhail Gorbachev.*

COUVERTURES USED: *Callebaut couverture from Belgium.*

Switzerland and France or other places make the same taste, the same shape year after year." He is so passionate about his metier, that he often works 16 and 18 hours a day, never turning down commissions, which he believes are challenging and inspirational. Schmidt's nocturnal activities sound like something out of a fairy tale: no one, except his partner Audrey Ryan, has ever seen him working on the chocolate creations that appear by day in the shop. After everyone has left the building, Joseph sets to work, mixing his palate of many-colored chocolates, and sculpting masterpieces which have been compared to Michelangelo, Rodin, and Matisse. His pieces range from exquisite miniatures to gigantic sculptures that have included a perfectly scaled-down version of a San Francisco cable car, three feet high, with every detail made in chocolate, commissioned for Queen Elizabeth II when she visited San Francisco.

Schmidt does not believe in incorporating nonedible structural supports, and he adores chocolate as a medium because it hardens in minutes, lasts for years, and because it also happens to be wonderful to eat. Schmidt will never, ever be a starving artist. His non-conformist style of working has resulted in the invention of many new techniques which he is in the process of trying to patent. Schmidt does not use tempering machines, instead opting for a series of plastic buckets, an old pastry oven, and the use of a pilot light. As he says, "I've been pushing my fingers into so much chocolate, it's now in my blood I think". Another endearing quality is that he does not take himself too seriously: "It's really exciting; I love it. When you have fun it shows." And it certainly does.

TASTING NOTES:

Slicks, an assortment of thin glossy disks, are beautifully crafted with decorations painted onto them in colors. The orange slick was white chocolate with a tangy orange butter ganache. Another highlight was the caramel in milk chocolate. The chocolate was very crisp, and the center moist, smooth, and well balanced. The couverture was good with no artificial flavorings.

The Schmidt's white chocolate mushroom was really good, not too sweet or cloying, and on the inside was a dark very smooth truffle, with a hint of Amaretto.

LA FONTAINE AU CHOCOLAT

101 & 210 RUE SAINT HONORÉ, 75001 PARIS, FRANCE
TEL: (33-1) 42 44 11 66/(33-1) 42 33 09 09
FAX: (33-1) 42 44 11 60

These two shops are owned by the Cluizel family. The first, opened by Michel Cluizel in 1987 in the rue Saint Honoré is famous for its chocolate "fountain"—a cascade of molten chocolate that tumbles down three copper steps. The shop is a showcase for Cluizel's chocolate, which is manufactured on a small industrial scale and is widely available throughout France.

The company started in 1947 in Damville, Normandy, when retired pastry chef, Marc Cluizel converted the laundry room into a chocolate production area. The following year, his 14-year-old son, Michel, joined him as his first employee. These days Michel Cluizel's two daughters and two sons work with him in the business.

This is one of the last independent French family-run businesses in the chocolate industry that still

*Michel Cluizel's 72 percent cocoa
bean chocolate bar.*

makes its own chocolate starting from the bean
and is probably best known for its 99 percent
cocoa-bean chocolate bar, which has many
devotees. It is not easy to detect any fine flavors as
the cocoa beans have been very highly roasted.

USEFUL INFORMATION:

STAR RATING: ★★
COUNTRY OF ORIGIN: *France*
AVAILABILITY: *Widely available, also from
branches. Mail order.*
BOX SIZES: *10 ounces, 14 ounces, 1¼
pounds, 1¾ pounds, 2¼ pounds, and 4½
pounds.*
HOUSE SPECIALTIES: *Chocolate bars,
autumn boxes filled with seasonal promotions.*
COUVERTURES USED:
*Made in-house using beans from Venezuela,
Ecuador, Brazil and Columbia, Ghana, Ivory
Coast, and Java.*

TASTING NOTES:

*The most interesting and successful creation to
date is undoubtedly the praline Saint-Roch—a
crunchy praline. The unexpected crunch comes
from fragments of unrefined, roasted cocoa beans,
and the flavor and texture are unique—I don't
suppose that many people have ever chewed on a
roasted cocoa bean, certainly an unforgettable
experience.*

*Also very beautifully packaged in a trompe
l'oeil bird's-eye maple box, there was a very
dramatic glittery palet argent with lots of silver
leaf and filled with a bitter but smooth and
buttery ganache; and a green-foil wrapped grape
soaked in Marc (white alcohol made from grapes)
with very bitter chocolate.*

*I also tasted a milk chocolate ganache with
rum soaked raisins which was very good; a sweet
fluffy praline in rich bitter chocolate; the Palet
Cacao de Brésil—a light marshmallowy ganache
that revealed burnt cocoa at the finish; and Palet
Cacao de Java—a whipped, buttery truffle, with
a rich chocolatey flavor.*

LE CHOCOLATIER
BRUYERRE

CHAUSEE DE BRUXELLES, 47, B 6401 GOSSELIES,
BELGIUM
TEL: (32-71) 85 22 42/85 38 18   FAX: (32-71) 85 33 38

hocolatier and pâtissier Monsieur F. L. Bruyerre started as a baker and confectioner in 1909 and in 1910 began his chocolate business, which did well until 1940 when World War II broke out in Belgium. Monsieur Bruyerre died in 1944, leaving behind two daughters, who had married two brothers: E. and A. Collet. At this time they had to make a decision whether to take the path of producing chocolate bars or artisan chocolates. Choosing the latter, they have developed over the years and now produce high-quality handmade chocolates for the domestic and export markets.

The maître chocolatier is 52-year-old Jean-Marie Poty, who sold his own business to become overall production and personnel manager.

USEFUL INFORMATION:

STAR RATING: ★

COUNTRY OF ORIGIN: *Belgium*

AVAILABILITY: *From the branch at Gosselies, Brussels, also Paris, Cologne, London, New York, and Tokyo.*

BOX SIZES: *Box or ballotin sizes 8 ounces, 1 pound, and 2¼ pounds.*

HOUSE SPECIALTIES: *Three lines of chocolates: Classic, Prestige and Maître Chocolatier, as well as truffles, liqueurs, marzipans, and chocolate spreads.*

COUVERTURES USED: *Callebaut top quality couverture.*

LINDT & SPRÜNGLI

SEESTRASSE 204, CH-8802 KILCHBERG, SWITZERLAND
TEL: (41-1) 716 22 33   FAX: (41-1) 715 39 85

Lindt is one of the oldest Swiss chocolate companies, and its founder Rudolphe Lindt (1855-1909) was to revolutionize the manufacture of chocolate with his invention—the conching (or refining machine). This machine enabled the particles of chocolate to be ground so finely that, with the addition of cocoa butter, the first melt-in-the-mouth chocolate bar was born. One of the other great Zurich chocolate families, the Sprünglis, took over the factory when Johann Rudolphe Sprüngli left his brother to run the famous chocolate shop. The trademark and rights were bought for the vast sum of one and a half million gold francs; and the company of Lindt and Sprüngli AG came into existence. These days the company produces a huge variety of chocolate bars, assortments, eggs, and couvertures, to a very high specification.

USEFUL INFORMATION:

STAR RATING: ★ ★

COUNTRY OF ORIGIN: *Switzerland*

AVAILABILITY: *Specialty stores, supermarkets, and duty-free shops worldwide.*

BOX SIZES: *Numerous*

HOUSE SPECIALTIES: *Grand Cru bars; Lindor cornets, Lindt Orange thins, and Easter eggs.*

COUVERTURES USED:

Their own, made to own unique and original recipe using bean varieties from Trinidad, Grenada, and Ghana.

$\mathcal{M}$AZET DE $\mathcal{M}$ONTARGIS

PLACE MIRABEAU, MONTARGIS, FRANCE
TEL: (33) 38 98 63 55

Legend has it that the praline was the result of an accident in a kitchen in 1671. The Duke of Plessis Praslin, known for his love of good food, was waiting impatiently for his dessert, and unfortunately, or perhaps fortunately, the clumsy kitchen boy had dropped a bowl full of almonds onto the floor. The enraged chef went to box his ears and managed to compound the problem by spilling a pan of hot burnt sugar over the almonds. The Duke smelled a delicious aroma wafting into the dining room and demanded to taste this new confection. He was so delighted that he modestly coined them "Praslin." Since then, this delicacy has undergone many changes, but can still be recognized in its original form, as made by Mazet de Montargis from the original secret recipe. Other variations known as praline can be found in evidence throughout the chocolate world.

(left) House truffles
(right) The original Praslines

The Confisserie du Roy, in existence in Montargis since 1647 and famous for its "praslin," was bought in 1902 and its name changed to Mazet de Montargis. The third generation of the family still owns and runs the beautiful historic shop in Montargis and one in Paris.

TASTING NOTES:

The house specialties include a selection of truffles and chocolates, and they also have fruit paste, almond paste, and marron glacés. Their Praslines are caramelized grilled almonds.

Amandas were almond nougatine dipped in chocolate and cocoa; and Mirabos, a filbert and orange nougat covered with milk chocolate and cocoa.

Other nutty specialties were Passions—chocolate-covered sugared almonds; Lyette—chocolate-covered sugared filberts; Grelons—sugared filberts covered in milk chocolate and sugar; and Givrettes—sugared almonds covered in milk chocolate.

NEUHAUS

POSTBOX 2, B-1602 VLEZENBEEK, BELGIUM
TEL: (32-2) 568 2211   FAX: (32-2) 568 2207

*N*euhaus is surely one of the most famous Belgian chocolate makers. Dating back to 1857, it was started by Jean Neuhaus, a Swiss who settled in Belgium, and who claims to have invented the "praline." Neuhaus opened his first shop, which was, in fact, an apothecary, with his brother-in-law. Marshmallows, licorice, and squares of chocolate were sold as aids to digestion. After his brother-in-law died, Neuhaus developed the chocolate side of the business, which rapidly gained a reputation for fine confectionery. Among the famed specialties were fruit pastes, vanilla chocolate, caramels, and "praslines," a kind of caramelized almond without chocolate. 1895 saw the opening of the first exclusive chocolate shop "Neuhaus—Jerrin." The business was kept in the family and passed down the generations until 1978 when it was sold and developed into the multinational business NV Neuhaus Mondose SA.

Neuhaus's flagship shop in Belgium.

TASTING NOTES:

These are mass-produced and machine-made chocolates that smell very sweet and are large in size. White chocolate dominates the selection. There was good dark couverture on the dark oval with "Neuhaus" on it that had several layers of avocaat cream that was very sweet, fluid and buttery—a rum truffle.

The dark "N" had crunchy nuts and a praline layer; an elongated chocolate had a crunchy layer and a white vanilla Montelimar center with a crystalline center, whipped butter icing center; and a white chocolate, a "fresh cream" center that was also very sweet.

USEFUL INFORMATION:

STAR RATING: ★

COUNTRY OF ORIGIN: *Belgium*

AVAILABILITY: *65 shops in Belgium, others in Europe, U.S., Canada, Japan, Hong Kong, and Australia.*

BOX SIZES: *Numerous*

HOUSE SPECIALTIES: *Caprice, Tentation, Marron, truffles, chocolates made with fresh cream and alcohol, plus 65 varieties of praline.*

COUVERTURES USED:
Callebaut

$\mathscr{P}$UYRICARD

QUARTIER BEAUFORT, 13090 PUYRICARD, FRANCE
TEL: (33) 42 96 11 21   FAX: (33) 42 21 47 10

$\mathscr{B}$elgians by birth, Marie-Anne and Jean-Guy Roelandts came from the Belgian Congo to the Provençal village of Puyricard in 1968. Without any chocolate tradition in their family other than a vacation course in Brussels, they set about learning a new trade and converting the locals, for whom chocolate at that time was only on the fringe of their gastronomic traditions, and eaten sparingly only at Christmas. Marie-Anne was in charge of the chocolate, while Jean-Guy took on the difficult task of changing local provençal tastes. Some 27 years later, Puyricard has increased from a two person production team to one boasting 26 maître chocolatiers, 70 full-time staff (200 around Christmas), and 11 shops in France supervised by Madame Roelandts. The business looks set to remain a

STAR RATING: ★ ★

COUNTRY OF ORIGIN: *France*

AVAILABILITY: *From shops in France.
Worldwide mail order.*

BOX SIZES: *Ballotins 8 ounces to 2¼
pounds. Also special export boxes New York 1
pound which holds 36 pieces; and Los Angeles
1½ pounds which holds 60 pieces.*

HOUSE SPECIALTIES: *A very wide range
of chocolates, 92 different varieties in all. Most
of the chocolates are hand-molded rather than
enrobed, and any foil wrapping is also done by
hand. Two Provençal specialties are the Clou
de Cézanne (Cézanne's nail), a crystallized fig
and marc de Provence in a C-shaped chocolate;
and Lou Poutounet (a little kiss), a light filbert
praline in milk or dark chocolate. A seasonal
specialty (mainly for the summer as it gets very
hot and chocolate sales slow down) is the
Calisson—a typical sweetmeat from this area of
Provence. It is made from the local almonds
and candied fruits or melon and orange peel
and lemon juice in flat oval shapes with royal
icing on top and rice paper underneath.*

COUVERTURES USED:

*Made especially by Callebaut. The milk is
made from Javan or Madagascan beans, the
dark from South and Central American
criollo and trinitario beans blended with a
little African forastero.*

family affair as the Roelandts' son and daughter have joined the team.

Despite her initial grounding in the Belgian tradition, Marie-Anne Roelandts has turned against what she perceives as the overuse of sugar, fats, and the poor quality of raw materials used in her home country. Although the recipes she uses are similar to Belgian ones, the low sugar content is the major distinguishing factor. It is this break with tradition that she feels has led to her success. Using no long-life cream, dehydrated butter, preservatives, or freezing, she says, "I want to arrive at a quality of 100 percent. Others may be happy with 70 percent and everything's OK. But that doesn't interest me at all."

TASTING NOTES:

*In the well-presented box, the chocolates looked
superb, gleaming and in tiptop condition. A high
proportion were molded shells, which are favored
because it means very light and fluid centers can
be used to fill the chocolates. In spite of the
praiseworthy lack of sugar, these chocolates owe a
great deal to the Belgian tradition in terms of
their couvertures and fillings. I found the
chocolate itself very smooth. I tasted the very
smooth and buttery palet d'or, a milk chocolate
heart, and the caramel, marzipan, and pralines,
which were all very rich and well made.*

ℛAMÓN ℛOCA
𝒞HOCOLATES

MERCADERS, 6 17004, GERONA, SPAIN
TEL: (34-72) 203662/201736   FAX: (34-72)206337

This large chocolate-producing company was founded by the Roca family in 1928. Ramón Roca Vinals is one of the company's two maître chocolatiers. He has been working with chocolate for 42 years, attending courses in Paris, Zurich, Kalmar, Lyon, and Brussels. His master craftsmanship has won him many prizes at international competitions, where he has shown some of his chef d'oeuvres in chocolate such as The Thinker, 5ft. 3in. tall, after the French sculpture by Rodin; the Discobolo, 6ft. after Miron; a 7ft. Statue of Liberty; and a life-size model of Christopher Columbus.

Checkers set in white and dark chocolate.

The other maître chocolatier is Ramón Roca Miralles, who has had 15 years' experience in chocolate making, studying in Paris, Geneva, Zurich, Lyon, Rome, Kalmar, and Brussels. Following in the chocolate art tradition, he has reproduced in chocolate The Creation Tapestry, in the 12th century Girona Cathedral, and some of the paintings of Dali, Picasso, Miro, Toulouse Lautrec, and Van Gogh.

USEFUL INFORMATION:

STAR RATING: ★

COUNTRY OF ORIGIN: *Spain*

AVAILABILITY: *From branches in Spain, Japan, U.S., Britain, Holland, Germany, and Italy.*

BOX SIZES: *Not applicable.*

HOUSE SPECIALTIES: *The company has a whimsical range of chocolate novelties including a cleverly designed set of checkers in white and dark chocolate, as well as backgammon, dominoes, and chess sets. The seasonal specialties is marrons glacés.*

COUVERTURES USED:

Dark 62 percent, milk 35 percent, and white 32 percent.

ROGERS' CHOCOLATES

913 GOVERNMENT STREET, VICTORIA, BRITISH
COLUMBIA, CANADA V8W 1X5
TEL: (604) 384-7021, (800) 663-2220 FOR MAIL ORDER
FAX: (604) 384-5750

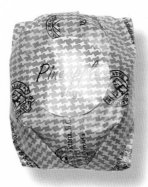

Charles "Candy" Rogers, who started out over 100 years ago as a vegetable grocer who also sold imported candies from San Francisco, found his source of supply unreliable, so decided to try his hand at producing his own confections. The story goes that they were so popular, long lines formed each morning before the shop opened, while in the kitchen at the back of the store, Rogers, clad only in red underwear, stirred copper kettles full of fondant candy. "Candy" Rogers developed a line of chocolates and candies, and is famed for his Victoria creams. His store, built in 1903, remains charmingly intact, with its antique cabinets and beveled glass counters.

When Rogers died, his wife took over the business until the late 1920s, and there have been several owners since then. In the last 10 years, under the current owners, the business has expanded

STAR RATING: ★

COUNTRY OF ORIGIN: *Canada*

AVAILABILITY: *Sold in 300 outlets in Canada including Eaton's and the Hudson Bay Company. Worldwide mail order and can be ordered through E-mail.*

BOX SIZES: *From 6 ounces to 2 pounds for the creams.*

HOUSE SPECIALTIES: *Victoria creams, dark chocolate almond brittle, chocolate-coated ginger, chocolate mint wafers, butterscotch crunch, and Empress squares. Seasonal specialties for Valentine's Day, Mother's Day, Easter, and Halloween are available only at the Victoria retail outlets.*

COUVERTURE USED: *Guittard*

dramatically from 2 stores and 3 wholesale customers to 300 wholesale and 25,000 mail-order clients. Some chocolates are still made in the kitchen at the back of the store, but most are produced at a factory outside Victoria. The company has introduced machinery to cope with demand and now has 50 employees.

The maître chocolatier is also the Plant Manager, Brian Boychuk. With extensive experience in food technology and microbiology, he has carried out extensive studies into the use and properties of various chocolates.

TASTING NOTES:

I tasted the Victorian creams, which looked fresh, glossy, and handmade. They were well-made fondants in a variety of flavors including rum and nut, pecan, and peach, coated in very good smooth bittersweet chocolate.

$\mathscr{S}$PRÜNGLI

BAHNHOFSTRASSE 21, 8022 ZURICH, SWITZERLAND
TEL: (41-1) 211 5777   FAX: (41-1) 211 3435

$\mathscr{S}$prüngli, not to be confused with Lindt & Sprüngli, must be one of the oldest and most famous chocolate establishments in the world. It was started in 1836 by David Sprüngli and is still run by the family today, now into the sixth generation of Sprünglis. The 60-year-old David Sprüngli acquired Vogel's confectioners in Martgasse from the widow Vogel, whose shop had been in existence since 1720, and, with his 20-year-old son Rudolf, founded Confiserie Sprüngli. In 1859, the shop relocated to Paradeplatz, now in the center of the famous shopping area. By 1870 the chocolate side of the business had outgrown the small atelier in the shop premises on Paradeplatz, so production moved to Werdmuhle.

In 1892, Rudolf Sprüngli divided the two sides of the business between his two sons, Johann Rudolf Sprüngli who took over the chocolate factory, now known as Lindt and Sprüngli, and David Robert Sprüngli who continued the confec-

TOP-TEN-SPRÜNGLI

tionery business in the Paradeplatz. The original building was reconstructed in 1909, and the very first tea room in Zurich opened. In those days it was uncommon for ladies to go anywhere without a male escort, and Sprüngli can be held partly responsible for the relaxing of this tradition, in giving the ladies of Zurich an opportunity to take tea or chocolate with their friends away from the rarefied atmosphere of their homes. Today the café is as popular as ever, being THE place to meet. It still offers a unique opportunity to indulge in the array of cakes and to exchange hot gossip.

Sprüngli clings to its tradition of artisan-produced chocolates and cakes, and although the production is now geared to vast quantities, the attention to detail and the quality of the raw ingredients remains the core philosophy; only the best and freshest ingredients are used. Their celebrated Truffes du Jour are produced daily from chocolate, cream, and butter; they are guaranteed never to be more than 24 hours old. Thanks to over 150 years of expertise in the field of chocolate making, Sprüngli has a finely tuned stock-control system, which is almost instinctive —rarely do they run out, and overproduction is unusual.

Sprüngli is also most thoughtful concerning any Zurich ex-patriots and other aficionados of their delicious confections. Parcels of chocolate mailed to destinations all over the world are guaranteed to arrive within 24 hours of their despatch. A flourishing relationship between Sprüngli and Federal Express has helped to boost exports in this specialist and rapidly expanding area of the business.

TORRAS

CTRA. GIRONA BARCELONA, KM.15, 17844 CORNELLA
DE TERRI, GIRONA, SPAIN
TEL: (34-972) 58 10 00   FAX: (34-972) 58 09 09

*T*orras is probably best known for its Xocolata a la Pedra or stone ground chocolate, with cinnamon and cornstarch—a throwback to the early days of Spanish colonial chocolate in the early 17th century. The packaging is a beautifully simple brown paper wrapper, which belies the fact that Torras is one of Spain's largest chocolate producers. Although these products are made on an industrial scale, some retain a pioneering spirit and simplicity, while others are bang up to date and positively innovative, the chocolate fondue being an obvious example. It is packed in an earthenware dish, with a plastic lid, and instructions for melting in the microwave —a brilliant piece of marketing.

The company was founded in 1890 by Señora Dolores Torras, and she started out producing 220 lbs. of chocolate a day. In 1924 the company was bought by the Costa Family.

Drinking chocolate, chocolate bars, and chocolate fondue.

More than 40,000 visitors are received every year by Torras, ranging from school children and students to business people, and apart from seeing the whole production process, they can also visit the collection of animals in the company's private zoo! Now owned by the Sans family, the company has begun exporting a selection of exciting new products such as Chocolate Fondue.

TASTING NOTES:

The Xocolata a la Pedra, made according to the instructions on the packet, produced several excellent cups of rich and spicy drinking chocolate. Heartily recommended!

Index